ANCIENT COINS IN NORTH AMERICAN COLLECTIONS

THE JOHN MAX WULFING COLLECTION IN WASHINGTON UNIVERSITY

By KEVIN HERBERT

ANCIENT COINS IN NORTH AMERICAN COLLECTIONS

PUBLISHED BY

THE AMERICAN NUMISMATIC SOCIETY

NEW YORK 1979

ISBN 0-89722-180-X

COMPOSED IN BELGIUM AT CULTURA, WETTEREN

PRINTED IN THE UNITED STATES OF AMERICA

FOREWORD

John Max Wulfing (1859-1929) made a lifelong avocation of collecting Greek, Roman, and Byzantine coins, and in the year before his death he donated his cabinet of many thousands of pieces to the Department of Classics of Washington University. Wulfing was primarily interested in the Roman coinage, both Republican and Imperial, but the Greek coins in his collection also received his devoted attention. As the present work abundantly reveals, he expended great effort to acquire issues of high quality from every area and period of the Greek world.

The author wishes to thank Mr. John H. Biggs, Vice Chancellor for Financial Affairs of the University, and Mr. Christian Baird Peper of St. Louis for their encouragement and generous support in bringing this project to its completion. He also sincerely thanks Mrs. Hyla A. Troxell of The American Numismatic Society for her expert editorial assistance with recent bibliography and other matters in the preparation of the manuscript.

All weights are in grams and all coins are silver unless otherwise indicated. Finally, all photographs of the coins were made by the undersigned.

The John Max Wulfing Collection is published by The American Numismatic Society as part of its continuing commitment to record in print material of numismatic value which is not readily accessible to researchers.

Kevin Herbert
Professor of Classics and
Curator of Coins
Washington University
St. Louis, Missouri

GALLIA: MASSALIA

Obv. Male head.
Rev. MA in two quarters of wheel.

1. 0.75. Obol.
2. 0.68. Obol.

MEDIOMATRICI

Obv. Male head.
Rev. Pegasus; below, two groups of three pellets and uncertain symbol; in exergue, two connected rows of pellets.

3. ↓ 2.04. AV quarter stater.

GERMANIA: VINDELICI

Obv. Shell pattern; to either side, pellet; all partially surrounded by chevrons.
Rev. Six pellets forming a triangle.

4. 7.42. AV stater.

ETRURIA: UNCERTAIN MINT

Obv. Wheel with six spokes.
Rev. Head of bipennis; to r., ✓ (?).

5. 5.32. Æ semuncia.

SAMNIUM: AESERNIA

Obv. Head of Vulcan wearing wreathed pileus; to l., traces of VOVCA-NOM; to r., tongs.
Rev. Traces of AISERNINO. Zeus driving biga; above, flying Nike.

6. ↑ 6.41. Æ litra.

CAMPANIA: CALES

Obv. Head of Athena wearing crested Corinthian helmet with crested serpent on bowl; to r., owl.
Rev. CALENO Nike driving biga.

7. ↓ 7.15. Didrachm.

Obv. CALENO Laureate head of Apollo.
Rev. CALENO Man-headed bull; above, cithara.

8. ↓ 6.45. Æ.

Obv. Head of Athena wearing crested Corinthian helmet.
Rev. CALENO Cock; to l., star.

9. ↗ 6.49. Æ.

CUMAE

Obv. Female head.
Rev. KYMAION, retrograde. Mussel-shell; above, barleycorn.

10. ↘ 6.12. Didrachm.

HYRIA

Obv. Head of Athena wearing Attic helmet with wreath and owl on bowl.
Rev. YDINA Man-headed bull.

11. → 6.85. Didrachm.

NEAPOLIS

Obv. Diademed female head.
Rev. ΝΕΟΠΟΛΙΤΩΝ Man-headed bull; above, flying Nike.

12. ↖ 7.10. Didrachm. *Obv.* to l., grapes. *Rev.* below, ⩎.
13. ↑ 7.18. Didrachm. *Obv.* around head, four dolphins. *Rev.* ethnic off flan; below, ΟΥΙΛ.
14. ↙ 7.25. Didrachm. *Obv.* to l., grapes; below, ΣΤΑ; to r., Χ. *Rev.* below, K.
15. ↗ 6.88 Didrachm. As 14.

Obv. Traces of ΝΕΟΠΟΛΙΤΩΝ. Laureate head of Apollo; to r., Γ.
Rev. Man-headed bull; above, flying Nike; below, ΙΣ; in exergue, trace of uncertain monogram.

16. ← 6.11. Æ.

SUESSA AURUNCA

Obv. Laureate head of Apollo; to r., O.
Rev. SVESANO Man-headed bull; above, flying Nike.

17. ↓ 6.20. Æ.

Obv. Head of Athena wearing crested Corinthian helmet.
Rev. SVESANO Cock; to l., star.

18. ↓ 7.41. Æ.

APULIA: ARPI

Obv. Laureate head of Zeus; to l., ΔΑΙΟΥ; to r., traces of fulmen.
Rev. Traces of ΑΡΠΑΝΩΝ. Boar; above, spear.

19. ↓ 8.47. Æ.

VENUSIA

Obv. ꟼE Veiled head of Hera; to r., three pellets.
Rev. Three crescents, each containing a star.

20. 10.21. Æ quadrans.

CALABRIA: BRUNDISIUM

Obv. Laureate head of Poseidon; to l., trident and traces of Nike.
Rev. BRVN Youth riding dolphin and holding Nike and cithara.

21. ↖ 8.51. Æ reduced semis. *Obv.* below, ∽.

22. ↗ 4.42. Æ reduced triens. *Obv.* below, four pellets. *Rev.* below, four pellets.

TARENTUM

A. J. Evans, "The 'Horsemen' of Tarentum," *NC* 1889, pp. 1–228.

O. E. Ravel, *Descriptive Catalogue of the Collection of Tarantine Coins Formed by M. P. Vlasto* (London, 1947).

Obv. TARAϟ, retrograde. Dolphin rider; below, scallop-shell.
Rev. Wheel with four spokes.

23. 7.98. Didrachm. Vlasto 75 (same dies).

Obv. Dolphin rider holding sepia.
Rev. Traces of TARAϟ, retrograde. Hippocamp; below, scallop-shell.

24. ← 8.11. Didrachm. Vlasto 113 (same dies).

Obv. Mounted rider (mounted Dioscuri on 29).
Rev. ΤΑΡΑΣ Taras riding dolphin.

Evans Period III, ca. 380–345 B.C.

25. ↙ 7.91. Didrachm. *Obv.* below, Θ. Vlasto 449–52, 454.

Evans Period V, ca. 334–330 B.C.

26. → 7.81. Didrachm. *Obv.* rider lances downward, holding shield and two javelins behind; to l., Ξ; below, ΑΡΙ. *Rev.* Taras holds cantharus (mostly off flan) and oar; below, ΚΛ. Vlasto 636–37.

Evans Period VII, ca. 281–272 B.C.

27. ↘ 6.21. Reduced didrachm. *Obv.* rider as on 26; to l., ΓΥ; below, traces of ΣΩΣΤΡΑΤΟΣ. *Rev.* Taras holds Nike and cornucopiae; to l., traces of ΠΟΛΥ; to r., fulmen. Vlasto 714–19.

28. ← 6.51. Reduced didrachm. *Obv.* rider crowns horse; above, ΙΩ; below, ΝΕΥΜΗ. *Rev.* Taras holds horned helmet; to l., trace of star; to r., ΠΟΛΥ and star. Vlasto 739–45.

29. ↗ 6.27. Reduced didrachm. *Obv.* above, ☧; below, by horse's hooves, traces of ΣΩΔΑΜΟΣ. *Rev.* Taras holds Nike, shield adorned with hippocamp, and two lances; to l., traces of ΓΥ; below, waves. Vlasto 773–80.

30. ↗ 6.52. Reduced didrachm. *Obv.* rider wears cloak and crowns horse; below, by horse's hooves, traces of ΣΩΔΑΜΟΣ. *Rev.* Taras, l. arm draped, brandishes trident. Vlasto 784–85.

31. ← 6.09. Reduced didrachm. *Obv.* rider wears crested helmet and holds shield and two lances; to r., ΙΩ; below, traces of ΗΙ ΑΠΟΛΛΩ. *Rev.* Taras holds grapes and distaff; to r., ΑΝΘ. Vlasto 789–96.

32. ↘ 6.32. Reduced didrachm. *Obv.* rider crowns himself; to l., ΙΩ; below, ΙΑΛΟ and top of Ionic column. *Rev.* Taras holds aphlaston and distaff; to r., ΑΝΘ. Vlasto 806–7 (which have ΑΝΘ, not ΑΝ as described).

Evans Period VIII, ca. 272–235 B.C.

33. ↘ 6.39. Reduced didrachm. *Obv.* rider crowns horse; above, ΣΥ; below, ΛΥΚΙΝΟΣ. *Rev.* Taras as on 30; to r. owl. Vlasto 836–41.

34. ← 6.24. Reduced didrachm. *Obv.* rider crowns horse; above, ☧; below, bearded mask and (to r.) traces of ΚΥΝΩΝ. *Rev.* Taras holds cantharus. Vlasto 859–62 (with obverse name reported as ΚΙΝΩΝ; but see *SNGANS* Part I, nos. 1189 and 1192–93, which clearly have ΚΥΝΩΝ).

35. ↖ 6.66. Reduced didrachm. *Obv.* rider as on 34; above, ΦΙΛΟΚΡΑ; below, ΝΚ. *Rev.* Taras holds Nike (off flan) and trident; below, ΑΡΙΣΤΟ. Vlasto 868–71 (wrongly described with obverse markings on reverse) and 873–76.

36. ↖ 6.10. Reduced didrachm. *Obv.* rider gallops, holding javelin; below, ⊢ΙΠ-ΠΟΔΑ. *Rev.* Taras holds cantharus and distaff; to r.,ΔΙ and amphora (largely off flan). Vlasto 904–6.

Obv. Scallop-shell.
Rev. ΤΑΡΑΣ, retrograde. Dolphin; below, scallop-shell.

37. ↑ 0.70. Litra. Vlasto 1135-36 (*rev.* die of 1135).

Obv. Head of Athena wearing Attic helmet (crested Corinthian helmet on 43); on bowl, hippocamp (38-39), Scylla (40), olive wreath (41), or rosette and Triton? (42).
Rev. Herakles fighting lion.

38. ↖ 1.04. Diobol. *Rev.* possible traces of ΤΑΡ; to l., club; between Herakles' legs, possible trace of letter. Compare Vlasto 1254–59, 1261–62.

39. → 0.98. Diobol. *Rev.* above, Δ. Compare Vlasto 1290–94.

40. ↑ 0.94. Diobol. *Rev.* above, owl. Vlasto 1322–24.

41. ↙ 1.22. Diobol. *Rev.* Herakles holds club. Vlasto 1339–43.

42. ↑ 1.14. Diobol. *Rev.* below, Φ. Compare Vlasto 1360–61 (with obverse head l.).

43. → 1.05. Diobol. *Rev.* traces of ethnic; Herakles holds club; below lion, trace of owl. Vlasto 1431–35.

Obv. Scallop-shell.
Rev. Dolphin; below, crab.

44. ← 0.31. Hemiobol. Vlasto 1559.

LUCANIA: METAPONTUM

S. P. Noe, *The Coinage of Metapontum*, ANSNNM 32 (New York, 1927).

Obv. Μ⚡ΤΑ (ΜΕΤ on 48). Ear of barley.
Rev. Same type, incuse.

45. ↑ 8.03. Stater. Noe 74.

46. ↑ 7.90. Stater. Noe 97.

47. ↑ 8.10. Stater. Noe 185.

48. ↑ 7.41. Stater. Noe 197.

Obv. Head of Leucippus wearing Corinthian helmet; to l., lion's head; to r., Ā (off flan).
Rev. ΜΕΤΑ Ear of barley with leaf; to l., club and ΑΜΙ.

49. ↓ 9.21. Stater.

Obv. Head of Demeter.
Rev. ΜΕΤΑ Two ears of barley.

50. ↑ 4.51. Æ.

POSEIDONIA

Obv. ΠΟΜ (51), or ΠΟΜΕΣ, retrograde (52). Poseidon wearing chlamys and brandishing trident.
Rev. ΠΟΜ, retrograde. Same type, incuse.

51. ↑ 6.10. Stater.

Rev. ΠΟΜΕΣ, retrograde. Bull.

52. ↙ 7.85. Stater.

SYBARIS

Obv. ΜV, retrograde. Bull, looking back.
Rev. Same type, incuse.

53. ↑ 7.70. Stater.

THURIUM

Obv. Head of Athena wearing wreathed Attic helmet.

Rev. ΘΟΥΡΙΩΝ Bull; in exergue, fish.

54. ↙ 7.80. Stater.

VELIA

Obv. Female head; to l., Ǝ.

Rev. VEΛH Owl on olive branch.

55. ↗ 3.66. Drachm.

Obv. Head of Athena wearing Attic helmet; on bowl, griffin (wreath on 56).

Rev. YEΛHTΩN Lion stalking (56, 60) or attacking stag (57-59).

56. ↖ 8.05. Didrachm. *Obv.* to r., poorly preserved, owl. *Rev.* traces only of ethnic.

57. ↑ 7.29. Didrachm. *Obv.* to r., Γ. *Rev.* below, Θ.

58. ↙ 6.90. Didrachm. *Obv.* on helmet flap, Φ; to r., Ж. *Rev.* above, caduceus.

59. → 7.51. Didrachm. *Obv.* to l., A; to r., Φ. *Rev.* above, I, dolphin, and Φ.

60. ↖ 7.90. Didrachm. *Obv.* on helmet flap, palmette; to l., Φ; above, A; to r., IE. *Rev.* ethnic off flan.

BRUTTIUM: BRUTTII

The arrangement of the coins follows that proposed by H. Pfeiler in "Die Münzprägung der Brettier," *JNG* 1964, pp. 7-50. Individual coin references are to F. Scheu, "Bronze Coins of the Bruttians," *NC* 1961, pp. 51-66.

Obv. Head of bearded Ares wearing crested Corinthian helmet with griffin on bowl.

Rev. BPETTIΩN Nike crowning trophy.

61. ↗ 16.69. Æ double unit (reduceds extans). *Obv.* below, ear of barley; to r., two pellets. *Rev.* below, cornucopiae; above, possible trace of a second symbol. See Scheu 1–3.

62. ↙ 12.95. Æ double unit (reduced sextans). *Obv.* below, trace of harpa (?). *Rev.* below, anchor. See Scheu 11 (which also has ЖB to l. on reverse).

Obv. Diademed head of Nike; to l., NIKA.

Rev. BPETTIΩN Zeus hurling fulmen; below, star; to r., cornucopiae.

63. ↙ 3.83. Æ half unit. Scheu 27.

Obv. Head of bearded Ares wearing crested Corinthian helmet with griffin on bowl; below, hayfork (?).

Rev. BPETTIΩN Hera Hoplosmia, armed with helmet, spear, and shield; to r., traces of markings.

64. ↓ 15.29. Æ double unit (reduced sextans). Probably Scheu 55, with ꟻB and fulmen on reverse.

Obv. Laureate head of Zeus; to l., fulmen.

Rev. BPETTIΩN Ares fighting with spear and shield; to r., bucranium.

65. ↖ 7.80. Æ unit (reduced uncia). Scheu 45.

Obv. Diademed head of Nike.

Rev. BPETTIΩN Zeus driving biga; below, plow.

66. ↗ 3.99. Æ half unit. Scheu 128.

67. ↙ 3.41. Æ half unit. As 66.

CAULONIA

S. P. Noe, *The Coinage of Caulonia*, ANSNS 9 (New York, 1958).

Obv. KAVΛ, retrograde on 69. Apollo holding branch in r. hand and small running male figure or daimon, who also holds a branch, on l. arm; to r., stag, looking back.

Rev. Apollo and stag as on obverse, but incuse; smaller figure in outline.

68. ↑ 7.82. Stater. Noe 20 (same obv. die).

Rev. KAVΛO Stag.
69. ↘ 7.95. Stater. Noe 104.

Obv. Apollo holding branch in r. hand and with fillet hanging from outstretched l. arm; to l., ⫛.
Rev. Traces of KAVΛΩNIATAΣ. Stag.
70. ↗ 7.10. Stater. Noe 179.

CROTON

Obv. ϘΡΟ Tripod; below, two serpents.
Rev. Tripod, incuse.
71. ↑ 7.97. Stater.

Obv. ϘPOTON Tripod.
Rev. Flying eagle, incuse.
72. → 6.62. Stater.

Obv. ϘPO, retrograde. Tripod.
Rev. Sepia.
73. ↑ 1.05. Diobol. *Obv.* to r., ear of grain.
74. ↖ 1.03. Diobol. *Obv.* to r., heron.

Obv. Eagle on laurel branch.
Rev. KPO Tripod; to r., Δ.
75. ↑ 7.24. Stater.

HIPPONEUM = VIBO VALENTIA

Obv. Laureate head of Zeus; to l., trace of uncertain marking; to r., probable traces of ΔΙΟΣ.
Rev. ΕΙΠΟΝΙΕΩΝ Amphora; to r., torch.
76. → 6.02. Æ.

Obv. Diademed head of Hera; to l., S.
Rev. VALENTIA Double cornucopiae; to r., carnyx and S.
77. ← 4.65. Æ semis.

Obv. Laureate head of Apollo; to l., two pellets.
Rev. VALENTIA Cithara; to r., two pellets.
78. ↙ 2.38. Æ sextans.

RHEGIUM

Obv. Lion's scalp.
Rev. Traces of PHΓΙΝΩΝ. Laureate head of Apollo.
79. ↓ 7.80. Æ.

Obv. Laureate head of Apollo; to r., chelys (?).
Rev. PHΓΙΝΩΝ Tripod.
80. → 7.90. Æ.

Obv. Diademed head of Artemis.
Rev. PHΓΙΝΩΝ Cithara.
81. ↑ 6.68. Æ.

Obv. Janiform female head wearing polos.
Rev. PHΓΙΝΩΝ Asclepius seated, holding staff; to l., Π and tripod; in exergue, trace of serpent.
82. ↘ 8.18. Æ pentonkion.

Obv. Jugate heads of the Dioscuri wearing laureate pilei; above, two stars.
Rev. PHΓΙΝΩΝ Hermes wearing petasus and holding branch, caduceus, and cloak; to l., IIII and cornucopiae.
83. ← 3.31. Æ tetras.

Rev. PHΓΙΝΩΝ Asclepius, holding bird, branch, and staff; to l., IIII.
84. ↘ 2.67. Æ tetras.

TERINA

K. Regling, "Terina," *Programm zum Winckelmansfeste* 66 (Berlin, 1906).

Obv. Female head encircled by wreath.
Rev. TEPINAION Nike seated on overturned amphora, holding wreath and caduceus.
85. ↑ 7.62. Stater. Regling 7. Ca. 445–425 B.C.

Obv. Female head.
Rev. Nike seated on cippus, holding bird on outstretched hand; to r., Π.
86. ← 1.11. Sixth stater.

SICILY: AGRIGENTUM

The reference for no. 87 is the discussion of early Acragantine coinage, pp. 162–64, in the work cited below under Gela.

Obv. Traces of AK (above) and PA (below). Eagle; above, illegible graffito.
Rev. Crab; below, barleycorn.

87. ↙ 8.30. Didrachm. Jenkins Group IV. Ca. 490–480 B.C.

Obv. Eagle standing on hare.
Rev. AKPA, retrograde on 88. Crab.

88. ↑ 1.75. Hemidrachm. *Rev.* below, fish.
89. ← 2.03. Hemidrachm. *Obv.* to l., barleycorn. *Rev.* below, pistrix devouring fish.

AGYRIUM

Obv. Eagle; to l., olive spray.
Rev. Traces of ΑΓΥΡΙΝΑΙ. Wheel with four spokes.

90. 13.40. Æ.

CATANA

Obv. Quadriga; above, flying Nike.
Rev. KATAN[AION] Laureate head of Apollo.

91. ↘ 17.11. Tetradrachm.

Obv. Head of Dionysus wearing ivy wreath; to l., ΛΑΣΙΟ and possible traces of ΣΩ.
Rev. ΚΑΤΑΝΑΙΩΝ The two Catanaean brothers carrying their parents.

92. ↓ 4.43. Æ.

ENNA

Obv. Head of Demeter wearing grain wreath; to r., traces of ΔΑΜΑΤ.
Rev. Traces of ENN. Bull's head, horns filleted; above, barleycorn.

93. ↓ 12.45. Æ.

GELA

G. K. Jenkins, *The Coinage of Gela* AMUGS 2 (Berlin, 1970).

Obv. Mounted rider brandishing lance.
Rev. <ΕΛΑΣ Forepart of man-headed bull.

94. ↙ 8.10. Didrachm. Jenkins Group Ib, 35. Ca. 490/485–480/475 B.C.

HIMERA

Obv. Cock; to l., uncertain letters.
Rev. Incuse square of "mill-sail" pattern.

95. 5.16. Drachm.

LEONTINI

Obv. Quadriga; above, flying Nike.
Rev. ΛΕΟΝΤΙΝΟΝ (96) or ⋁ΕΟΝΤΙΝΟΝ (97). Lion's head; around, four barleycorns.

96. ↙ 17.44. Tetradrachm.

Obv. Laureate head of Apollo.

97. ↓ 17.47. Tetradrachm.

ZANCLE-MESSANA

H. E. Gielow, "Die Silberprägung von Dankle-Messana," *Mitteilungen der Bayerischen Numismatischen Gesellschaft* 48 (Munich, 1930), pp. 1–54.

Obv. ᗡANK⋁E Dolphin within sickle-shaped harbor.
Rev. Scallop-shell in center of geometrically patterned incuse square.

98. 5.71. Drachm. See Gielow 64 (same obv. die). Ca. 515–493 B.C.

Obv. Biga of mules; above, flying Nike; in exergue, two dolphins.
Rev. ΜΕΣΣΑΝΙΟΝ Running hare; below, dolphin.

99. ↘ 17.08. Tetradrachm.

MAMERTINI

The order follows that of M. Särström, *A Study in The Coinage of the Mamertines* (Lund, 1940).

Obv. Laureate head of young Ares; to l., spearhead; to r., ΑΡΕΟΣ.
Rev. ΜΑΜΕΡΤΙΝΩΝ Eagle on fulmen.

100. ↗ 7.74. Æ double unit. Särström IB.
101. ↗ 17.01. Æ quadruple unit. Särström IIIA.

Obv. Laureate head of Ares; to r., uncertain symbol.
Rev. ΜΑΜΕΡΤΙΝΩΝ Warrior with spear standing before horse; to l., Π.

102. → 10.80. Æ reduced pentonkion. Särström XIA.

Obv. Laureate head of Zeus; to l., uncertain symbol.
Rev. ΜΑΜΕΡΤΙΝΩΝ Helmeted warrior advancing with spear and shield; to r., Π.

103. ↙ 11.33. Æ reduced pentonkion. Särström XVIA.

NAXOS

H. A. Cahn, *Die Münzen der Sizilischen Stadt Naxos* (Basel, 1944).

Obv. Head of Dionysus wearing ivy wreath.
Rev. ΝΑΧΙ Squatting Silenus holding cantharus.

104. ↖ 4.21. Drachm. Cahn 57. Ca. 461–430 B.C.

SELINUS

Obv. Leaf of wild parsley.
Rev. Incuse square of "Union Jack" pattern.

105. 8.62. Didrachm.

SYRACUSE

Much attention has been paid to the Syracusan coinage in recent decades, and references especially pertinent to the Wulfing coins are cited below, together with the standard works. Non-traditional attributions, dates, and denominations derive from these newer studies.

Early Fifth Century B.C.

E. Boehringer, *Die Münzen von Syrakus* (Berlin, 1929).
C. M. Kraay, *Greek Coins and History* (London, 1969), pp. 19-42.

Obv. Horseman.
Rev. ΣΥϘΑΚΟΣΙΟΝ Head of Arethusa; around, four dolphins.

106. ← 8.52. Didrachm. Boehringer 99.

Obv. Quadriga; above, flying Nike.
Rev. ΣΥϘΑΚΟΣΙΟΝ, retrograde on 108. Head of Arethusa; around, four dolphins.

107. ↗ 17.30. Tetradrachm. Boehringer 113. Ca. 485–479 B.C. (Boehringer) or ca. 479–461 B.C. (Kraay).
108. ↘ 17.36. Tetradrachm. Boehringer 349. Dates as 107.

Late Fifth Century B.C.

Obv. ΣΥΡΑΚΟΣΙΩΝ (not preserved). Facing head of Athena, wearing triple-crested helmet; around, four dolphins.
Rev. ΣΥΡΑΚΟΣΙΩΝ Helmeted hero Leucaspis with shield and spear; behind to l., altar; behind to r., dead ram; in exergue (off flan), ΛΕΥΚΑΣΠΙΣ.

109. ↑ 3.72. Drachm.

Dionysius I

(No. 109 may also date from Dionysius' reign.)

C. F. Boehringer, "Zu Finanzpolitik und Münzprägung des Dionysios von Syrakus," *Greek Numismatics and Archaeology: Essays in Honor of Margaret Thompson*, ed. O. Mørkholm and N. M. Waggoner (New York, 1979), pp. 9-32.
A. Gallatin, *Syracusan Dekadrachms of the Euainetos Type* (Cambridge, Mass., 1930).
G. K. Jenkins, *The Coinage of Gela*, AMUGS 2 (Berlin, 1970).
C. M. Kraay, *Greek Coins* (London, 1966).
L. O. T. Tudeer, *Die Tetradrachmenprägung von Syrakus in der Periode der signierenden Künstler* (Berlin, 1913).

SICILY: SYACUSE (cont.)

Obv. Quadriga; above, flying Nike; in exergue, dolphin.
Rev. ΣΥΡΑΚΟΣΙΩΝ Head of Arethusa; around, four dolphins.

110. ↗ 16.49. Tetradrachm. Tudeer 98.

Obv. ΣΥΡΑ Head of Herakles wearing lion's skin headdress.
Rev. ΣΥΡΑ Quadripartite incuse square with head of Arethusa in center.

111. → 1.13. AV 1 1/3 litrae. Ca. 406–405 B.C. (Jenkins, pp. 99-100).

Obv. Quadriga; above, flying Nike; in exergue, armor.
Rev. ΣΥΡΑΚΟΣΙΩΝ (off flan). Head of Arethusa; around, four dolphins; to r., scallop-shell.

112. ↙ 43.22. Decadrachm. Merzbacher, 15 Nov. 1910, 262. *Obv.* Gallatin R.XI. *Rev.* Gallatin E.1, with developed flaws and some minor recutting, e.g., the addition of a tendril at the hairline near the corner of the eye. Ca. 395–370 B.C. (Kraay, p. 288).

Obv. ΣΥΡΑ Head of Athena wearing wreathed Corinthian helmet.
Rev. Sea-star between two dolphins.

113. ↗ 29.83. Æ drachm. Early fourth century (Boehringer).

Timoleon

Obv. Laureate head of Zeus Eleutherios; to r., traces of ΙΕΥΣ ΕΛΕΥΘΕΡΙΟΣ.
Rev. Free horse.

114. ↘ 19.33. Æ.

Agathocles

R. R. Holloway, "The Bronze Coinage of Agathocles," *Greek Numismatics and Archaeology: Essays in Honor of Margaret Thompson*, ed. O. Mørkholm and N. M. Waggoner (New York 1979), pp. 87-95.
G. K. Jenkins, "Electrum Coinage at Syracuse," *Essays in Greek Coinage Presented to Stanley Robinson*, ed. C. M. Kraay and G. K. Jenkins (Oxford, 1968) pp. 145-62.

Obv. Laureate head of Apollo.
Rev. ΣΥΡΑΚΟΣΙΩΝ Biga; below, triskeles.

115. ↖ 4.25. AV drachm.

Obv. Laureate head of Apollo; to r.. fulmen.
Rev. ΣΥΡΑΚΟΣΙΩΝ Tripod.

116. ↘ 3.44. EL 24 or 25 litrae. Jenkins Group B, 015–R32. Ca. 300 B.C.

Obv. Head of Persephone wearing grain wreath; to l., ΚΟΡΑΣ.
Rev. ΑΓΑΘΟΚΛΕΙΟΣ Nike building trophy; to l., triskeles.

117. ↗ 16.21. Tetradrachm.

Obv. ΣΥΡΑΚΟΣΙΩΝ (almost completely off flan). Head of Demeter wearing grain wreath; to r., poppy head.
Rev. Bull; above, dolphin and T; in exergue, dolphin.

118. ↙ 5.90. Æ hemilitron. Ca. 316 – ca. 310 B.C. or later (Holloway).

Obv. Head of Artemis; to r., ΣΩΤΕΙΡΑ.
Rev. ΑΓΑΘΟΚΛΕΟΣ ΒΑΣΙΛΕΟΣ Fulmen.

119. ↗ 8.33. Æ litra. 304 — late 290s B.C. (Holloway).

Obv. Traces of ΣΥΡΑΚΟΣΙΩΝ. Diademed head of Herakles; to r., star.
Rev. Lion raising forepaw; above, club; in exergue, ΣΩ.

120. ↖ 8.32. Æ litra. Late 290s–289 B.C. (Holloway).

Democracy

R. R. Holloway, "Eagle and Fulmen on the Coins of Syracuse," *RBN* 1962, pp. 5–28.

Obv. ΣΥΡΑΚΟΣΙΩΝ Head of Persephone wearing grain wreath; to l., ear of grain.

Rev. Biga; above, fulmen.

121. ↖ 7.62. Æ. Late 290s–288/287 B.C. (Holloway, pp. 10–16).

Hieron II

Obv. Veiled and diademed head of Queen Philistis.

Rev. ΒΑΣΙΛΙΣΣΑΣ ΦΙΛΙΣΤΙΔΟΣ Nike driving quadriga; above, crescent; to r., ΚΙ; below, ear of grain.

122. ↖ 13.48. 16 litrae.

Obv. Head of Hieron II, diademed (123) or laureate (124).

Rev. ΙΕΡΩΝΟΣ (off flan on 124). Mounted warrior with lance.

123. ↘ 17.22. Æ.

124. ← 17.71. Æ.

Obv. Diademed head of Poseidon.

Rev. ΙΕΡΩΝΟΣ Trident adorned with dolphins; below, ΑΝ.

125. ↖ 6.31. Æ.

Hieronymus

R. R. Holloway, *The Thirteen-Months Coinage of Hieronymos of Syracuse*, AMUGS 3 (Berlin, 1969).

Obv. Diademed head of Hieronymus.

Rev. ΒΑΣΙΛΕΩΣ ΙΕΡΩΝΥΜΟΥ Fulmen; above, Φ; below, Θ.

126. ↓ 10.09. Æ litra (?). See Holloway 66–72 (Series ΦΘ). Early 214 B.C.

TAUROMENIUM

Obv. Laureate head of Apollo; to l., ΑΡΧΑΓΕΤΑΣ.

Rev. ΤΑΥΡΟΜΕΝΙΤΑΝ Cithara.

127. ↗ 7.59. Æ.

Rev. ΤΑΥΡΟΜΕΝΙΤΑΝ Tripod.

128. ↑ 4.98. Æ.

ISLANDS OF SICILY: LIPARA

Obv. Laureate head of Ares.

Rev. ΛΙΠΑΡΑΙΩΝ Trident.

129. ↗ 6.94. Æ.

MACEDON: ACANTHUS

J. Desneux, "Les tétradrachmes d'Acanthos," *RBN* 1949, pp. 5–122.

Obv. Lion attacking bull; in exergue, floral ornament.

Rev. Quadripartite incuse square.

130. 17.25. Tetradrachm. See Desneux Type AA, 1 *bis*, dated to ca. 530–480 B.C. The unusually small flan and the strangely-shaped floral ornament of our coin connect it to Desneux's 1 *bis*. Both these anomalous coins also have reverse incuses which, although partially filled in, were originally divided by raised lines into four sub-squares. This type of incuse, however, is not found in Desneux's Types A–B, but starts only in his Type C. The placement of 1 *bis*, and that of our coin, is thus somewhat uncertain.

Obv. Forepart of bull, head turned back; above, flower.

Rev. Quadripartite granulated incuse square.

131. 2.24. Tetrobol.

AMPHIPOLIS

Obv. Diademed head of Artemis.

Rev. ΑΜΦΙΠΟΛΙΤΩΝ Two goats on hind legs facing each other.

132. ↑ 9.03. Æ.

Obv. Laureate head of Poseidon.

Rev. ΑΜΦΙΠΟΛ[ΙΤΩΝ] Bull; below, uncertain monograms.

133. ↑ 7.53. Æ.

BOTTIAEA

Obv. Macedonian shield with crescent-wheel in center.

Rev. ΒΟΤΤΕΑΤΩΝ Stern of galley; above, ΦΙ; below, ΔΙ.

134. 3.60. Drachm.

EION

Obv. Goose, head turned back; above, lizard.

Rev. Quadripartite incuse square.

135. 0.69. Trihemiobol.

LETE

Obv. Satyr with tail, and nymph; in center, pellet.
Rev. Incuse square.
136. 9.85. Stater.

MENDE

S. P. Noe, *The Mende (Kaliandra) Hoard*, ANSNNM 27 (New York, 1926).

Obv. Dionysus holding cantharus and reclining on back of ass.
Rev. ΜΕΝΔΑΙΟΝ framing vinestock with grape clusters.
137. ← 17.11. Tetradrachm. Noe 93. Ca. 450–423 B.C.

NEAPOLIS

Obv. Gorgoneion.
Rev. Rough quadripartite incuse square.
138. 8.41. Didrachm.

Rev. ΝΕΟΠ Female head.
139. ↖ 1.61. Triobol.

KINGS OF MACEDON: PHILIP II

G. Le Rider, *Les monnaies d'argent et d'or de Philippe II frappés en Macédoine de 359 à 294* (Paris, 1977).

Obv. Laureate head of Apollo.
Rev. ΦΙΛΙΠΠΟΥ Biga; below, fulmen.
140. ← 8.47. *AV* stater. Le Rider Pella II.1, 78. Ca. 340–328 or ca. 336–328 B.C.

Obv. Laureate head of Zeus.
Rev. ΦΙΛΙΠΠΟΥ Youthful horseman with palm branch; to r., rose.
141. ↗ 14.42. Tetradrachm. Le Rider Amphipolis IIA, 227. Ca. 348/7–343/2 B.C.

Obv. Head of Herakles wearing lion's skin headdress.
Rev. ΦΙΛΙΠΠΟΥ Fulmen.
142. ↓ 2.53. Æ.

ALEXANDER III

E. T. Newell, *Alexander Hoards II: Demanhur, 1905*, ANSNNM 19 (New York, 1923).

M. Thompson and A. R. Bellinger, "Greek Coins in the Yale Collection IV: A Hoard of Alexander Drachms," *Yale Classical Studies* 14 (New Haven, 1955), pp. 3–45.

Obv. Head of Athena in crested Corinthian helmet with serpent on bowl.
Rev. ΑΛΕΞΑΝΔΡΟΥ Nike holding wreath and stylis; to l., K; below ΗΡ (partially off flan).
143. ↙ 8.42. *AV* stater. Callatis. Posthumous. Attribution based on Newell's tray arrangement at the ANS.

Obv. Head of Herakles wearing lion's skin headdress.
Rev. ΑΛΕΞΑΝΔΡΟΥ (ΒΑΣΙΛΕΩΣ ΑΛΕΞΑΝΔΡΟΥ on 148 and 150). Zeus enthroned, holding eagle and sceptre.
144. ↖ 17.12. Tetradrachm. *Rev.* to l., Ε. Amphipolis. Newell 536. Ca. 328–327 B.C.
145. ↗ 17.04. Tetradrachm. *Rev.* to l., herm. Amphipolis. Newell 716. Ca. 328–327 B.C.
146. ← 17.18. Tetradrachm. *Rev.* to l., cock. Amphipolis. Newell 792. Ca. 328–327 B.C.
147. ↖ 17.15. Tetradrachm. *Rev.* to l., cornucopiae. Amphipolis. Newell 909. Ca. 326 B.C.
148. ↙ 17.30. Tetradrachm. *Rev.* to l., Phrygian cap. Amphipolis. Newell 1344. Ca. 324–323 B.C.
149. ↖ 16.92. Tetradrachm. *Rev.* to l., Λ and torch; below, star. Amphipolis. Posthumous. Attribution based on Newell's tray arrangement at the ANS.
150. ↑ 17.23. Tetradrachm. *Rev.* to l., wreath; below, ΔΙ. Phaselis or Side. Newell 1819.
151. ↑ 17.21. Tetradrachm. *Rev.* to l., forepart of ram; below, ΔΑ. Damascus. Newell 2919. Ca. 330–319 B.C.

152. ↙ 4.10. Drachm. *Rev.* to l., forepart of Pegasus; below, ΑΙ. Thompson-Bellinger, Lampsacus 14. 310 B.C., under Antigonus.

153. ↓ 4.04. Drachm. *Rev.* to l., [monogram] ; below, [monogram] . Thompson-Bellinger, Magnesia 21. 310 B.C., under Antigonus.

154. ↘ 3.92. Drachm. As 153.

Obv. Head of Herakles wearing lion's skin headdress.

Rev. ΑΛΕΞΑΝΔΡΟΥ Club and bow with quiver.

155. ↑ 5.33. Æ.

PHILIP III

References are those cited under Alexander III.

Obv. Head of Herakles wearing lion's skin headdress.

Rev. ΘΙΛΙΠΠΟΥ (ΒΑΣΙΛΕΩΣ ΦΙΛΙΠΠΟΥ on 156). Zeus enthroned, holding eagle and sceptre.

156. ↗ 17.13. Tetradrachm. *Rev.* to l., M; below, ΛΥ. Babylon. Newell 4526. Ca. 323–320 B.C.

157. ↑ 4.21. Drachm. *Rev.* to l., cithara; below, B. Thompson-Bellinger, Colophon 7. 319 B.C.

158. ↑ 4.10. Drachm. *Rev.* to l., [monogram]. Thompson-Bellinger, Colophon 8. 318 B.C.

159. ↗ 4.13. Drachm. *Rev.* to l., torch; below [monogram]. Thompson-Bellinger, Sardes 10. 322 B.C.

160. ↗ 4.04. Drachm. *Rev.* to l., torch; below, ΤΙ. Thompson-Bellinger, Sardes 12. 320 B.C.

DEMETRIUS POLIORCETES

E. T. Newell, *The Coinages of Demetrius Poliorcetes* (London, 1927).

Obv. Diademed and horned head of Demetrius.

Rev. ΒΑΣΙΛΕΩΣ ΔΗΜΗΤΡΙΟΥ Poseidon with trident, standing with one foot on rock; to l., [monogram] ; to r., [monogram] .

161. ↓ 16.92. Tetradrachm. Amphipolis. Newell 123 (obv. die CXIV, with minor recutting, of Newell 120). Ca. 289–288 B.C.

ANTIGONUS II GONATAS

Obv. Macedonian shield; in center, head of Pan with pedum at shoulder.

Rev. ΒΑΣΙΛΕΩΣ ΑΝΤΙΓΟΝΟΥ Athena Alkis; to l., Macedonian helmet; to r., [monogram] .

162. ↑ 17.12. Tetradrachm.

ANTIGONUS III DOSON

Obv. Head of Poseidon wearing seaweed wreath.

Rev. ΒΑΣΙΛΕΩΣ ΑΝΤΙΓΟΝΟΥ Apollo holding bow, seated on prow; below, [monogram] and [monogram].

163. ↖ 16.99. Tetradrachm.

PHILIP V

Obv. Diademed head of Philip.

Rev. ΒΑΣΙΛΕΩΣ ΦΙΛΙΠΠΟΥ Club in oak wreath; above, [monogram] ; below, [monogram] and M; to l., outside wreath, fulmen.

164. ↖ 3.51. Drachm.

Obv. Macedonian shield with wheel-device in center.

Rev. ΒΑ Φ Macedonian helmet.

165. 3.84. Æ.

TIME OF PHILIP V

Obv. ΜΑΚΕ Macedonian shield with club in center.

Rev. Macedonian helmet; to l., Σ and [monogram] ; to r., ΔΙ and trident.

166. ↙ 2.12. Tetrobol.

PERSEUS

A. Mamroth, "Die Silbermünzen des Königs Perseus," *ZfN* 1928, pp. 1-28.

Obv. Diademed head of Perseus.
Rev. ΒΑΣΙΛΕΩΣ ΠΕΡΣΕΩΣ Eagle on fulmen within oak wreath; above, [monogram]; to r., [monogram]; below, [monogram]; below, outside wreath, plow.

167. ↑ 13.76. Tetradrachm. Mamroth 23. Ca. 170–168 B.C.

MACEDONIA UNDER THE ROMANS

Obv. Macedonian shield; in center, diademed head of Artemis.
Rev. ΜΑΚΕΔΟΝΩΝ ΠΡΩΤΗΣ Club in oak wreath; above, [monogram]; below, [monogram] and [monogram]; to l., outside wreath, fulmen.

168. ↑ 16.90. Tetradrachm.
169. ↑ 16.90. Tetradrachm.

Obv. ΜΑΚΕΔΟΝΩΝ Head of Alexander the Great; to l., Θ.
Rev. AESILLAS Q Club between money chest and quaestor's chair; all in laurel wreath.

170. ↑ 16.31. Tetradrachm.
171. ↑ 16.10. Tetradrachm.

PAEONIAN KINGS: PATRAUS

Obv. Laureate male head.
Rev. ΠΑΤΡΑΟΥ (largely off flan). Horseman lancing fallen enemy, who holds Macedonian shield.

172. ↑ 12.82. Reduced tetradrachm.

TAURIC CHERSONESUS: PANTICAPAEUM

Obv. Head of satyr wearing ivy wreath.
Rev. ΠΑΝ Head of lion; below, sturgeon.

173. ↑ 6.72. Æ.

Rev. ΠΑΝ Bow and arrow.

174. ↗ 5.30. Æ.

SARMATIA: OLBIA

Obv. Gorgoneion.
Rev. ΟΛ Sea eagle on dolphin.

175. ↑ 19.66. Æ.

EUXINE DISTRICT: APOLLONIA PONTICA

Obv. Α Anchor; to r., crayfish.
Rev. Gorgoneion.

176. ← 3.23. Drachm.

ISTRUS

Obv. Two male heads facing and united, one inverted.
Rev. ΙΣΤΡΙΗ Sea eagle on dolphin; below, Δ.

177. ↙↗ 4.94. Drachm.

MESEMBRIA

Obv. Crested Corinthian helmet facing.
Rev. ΜΕΤΑ in four quarters of radiate wheel.

178. 1.38. Diobol.

THRACE: ABDERA

J. F. May, *The Coinage of Abdera*, ed. C. M. Kraay and G. K. Jenkins (London, 1966).

Obv. ΑΒΔΗΡΙΤΕΩΝ Recumbent griffin.
Rev. Laureate head of Apollo.

179. ↑ 10.02. Tetradrachm. *Rev.* ΕΠΙ ΔΙΟΦΑΝΤΟΥ. May Period IX, 539. Ca. 365/360–350/345 B.C.
180. ↖ 2.85. Drachm. *Rev.* illegible magistrate's name around shallow incuse square. May Period IX. Ca. 365/360–350/345 B.C.

BYZANTIUM

Obv. ϒΠ Cow standing on dolphin.
Rev. Quadripartite incuse square of "mill-sail" type.

181. 5.28. Siglos.
182. 2.48. Half-siglos. *Rev.* incuse surfaces granulated.

THRACIAN CHERSONESUS

Obv. Forepart of lion, looking back.
Rev. Quadripartite incuse square, with markings in two quarters.

183. 2.41. Light half-siglos (?). *Rev.* in each of two quarters, pellet.
184. 2.31. Light half-siglos (?). *Rev.* H and pellet.
185. 2.10. Light half-siglos (?). *Rev.* caduceus, and pellet and ΛΕ.
186. 2.21. Light half-siglos (?). *Rev.* Ā and I.

THRACIAN ISLANDS: THASOS

A. B. West, *Fifth and Fourth Century Gold Coins from the Thracian Coast*, ANSNNM 40 (New York, 1929).

Obv. Satyr carrying nymph.
Rev. Quadripartite incuse square.

187. 8.84. Stater.

Obv. Head of bearded Dionysus wearing ivy wreath.
Rev. ΘΑΣΙΟΝ Herakles kneeling, drawing bow.

188. ↙ 3.79. Drachm. West, Thasos 1a (this coin). Ca. 411–408, 404–390 B.C.

Rev. ΘΑΣΙΩΝ Club in wreath.

189. ↑ 1.61. Hemidrachm.

Obv. Head of young Dionysus wearing ivy wreath.
Rev. ΗΡΑΚΛΕΟΥΣ ΣΩΤΗΡΟΣ ΘΑΣΙΩΝ Herakles carrying club and lion's skin; to l., ΗΜ.

190. ↑ 16.55. Tetradrachm.
191. ↑ 16.07. Tetradrachm.

KINGS OF THRACE: LYSIMACHUS

M. Thompson, "The Mints of Lysimachus," *Essays in Greek Coinage Presented to Stanley Robinson*, ed. C. M. Kraay and G. K. Jenkins (Oxford, 1968), pp. 163–82.

Obv. Head of Herakles wearing lion's skin headdress.
Rev. ΒΑΣΙΛΕΩΣ ΛΥΣΙΜΑΧΟΥ Zeus enthroned, holding eagle and sceptre.

192. ↑ 17.01. Tetradrachm. *Rev.* to l., forepart of lion and torch; below, pentagram. Colophon. Thompson 122. 299/8–297/6 B.C.
193. ↑ 4.02. Drachm. *Rev.* to l., forepart of lion and crescent; below, pentagram. Colophon. Thompson 127. 299/8–297/6 B.C.

Obv. Diademed and horned head of Alexander the Great.
Rev. ΒΑΣΙΛΕΩΣ ΛΥΣΙΜΑΧΟΥ Athena seated with spear and shield, holding Nike.

194. ↑ 17.09. Tetradrachm. *Rev.* to outer l., star; to inner l., ΗΡ. Lampsacus. Thompson 46. 297/6–282/1 B.C.
195. ↗ 17.16. Tetradrachm. *Rev.* to inner l., caduceus with handle; to outer r., Κ. Amphipolis. Thompson 193. 288/7–282/1 B.C.
196. → 16.89. Tetradrachm. *Rev.* to inner l, [monogram]; in exergue ΗΡ. Amphipolis. Variant of Thompson 201 (with exergue monogram to outer r.). 288/7–282/1 B.C.

THESSALY: LAMIA

Obv. Head of young Dionysus wearing ivy wreath.
Rev. ΛΑΜΙΕΩΝ Amphora; to r., bow in case.

197. ↑ 2.39. Hemidrachm.

LARISSA

F. Herrmann, "Die Silbermünzen von Larissa in Thessalien," *ZfN* 1925, pp. 1–69.

Obv. Facing female head.
Rev. ΛΑΡΙΣΑΙΩΝ Horse grazing.

198. → 5.83. Drachm. Hermann Group VII, Series A. Ca. 395–344/3 B.C.

THESSALIAN CONFEDERACY

Obv. Head of Zeus wearing oak wreath.
Rev. ΘΕΣΣΑΛΩΝ Athena Itonia.

THESSALIAN CONFEDERACY (cont.)

199. ↑ 6.18. Double victoriate. *Obv.* ΝΙΚΟ-ΚΡΑΤΟΥΣ. *Rev.* above, ΦΙΛΟΞ-ΕΝΙΔΟΥ; in exergue, ΠΕΤΡΑΙΟΣ.
200. ↑ 6.16. Double victoriate. *Rev.* above, ΚΛΕΙΠΠΟΣ; in exergue, ΓΟΡΓΩ-ΠΑΣ.
201. ↗ 5.84. Double victoriate. *Obv.* ΞΕ-ΝΟΦ[ΑΝΤΟΣ]. *Rev.* above, in field, and in exergue, ΑΜΥΝΑΝΔΡΟΥ; to r. above, trace of owl; to r., Λ over Ⱶ. Markings restored from *SNGCop* Thessaly 288.

ILLYRICUM: APOLLONIA

Obv. Cow suckling calf, above, ΜΑΑΡ-ΚΟΣ; in exergue, [monogram].
Rev. ΑΠΟΛ Double stellate pattern; around, ΛΥΣΑΝΙΑ.
202. ↘ 2.79. Victoriate.

DYRRHACHIUM

Obv. Cow suckling calf.
Rev. ΔΥΡ Double stellate pattern.
203. ↑ 9.98. Stater. *Rev.* ethnic nearly illegible; to r., club.
204. ↘ 3.13. Victoriate. *Obv.* above, radiate head and ΦΙΛΩΝ. *Rev.* around, ΜΕΝΙΣΚΟΥ.

CORCYRA

Obv. ΚΟΡ Forepart of cow.
Rev. Grape cluster.
205. ↗ 2.51. Æ.

ACARNANIA

Corinthian-type staters of Leucas and Thyrrheium are catalogued after Corinth.

LOCRIS: LOCRI OPUNTII

Obv. Head of Demeter wearing grain wreath.
Rev. ΟΠΟΝΤΙΩΝ Helmeted Ajax with sword and shield; inside shield, serpent; at feet, crested Corinthian helmet and spear.
206. ↖ 11.69. Didrachm.

PHOCIS: FEDERAL COINAGE

R. T. Williams, *Silver Coinage of the Phokaians* (London, 1972).

Obv. Bull's head facing; above, Π.
Rev. ΦΟ[Κ]Ι Female head in shallow incuse square.
207. ↖ 3.55. Triobol. Williams Period III, Section 10, 164. Ca. 460–458/7 B.C. The weight is unusually high, yet the coin appears genuine.

BOEOTIA: HALIARTUS

Obv. Boeotian shield; on body of shield, trident.
Rev. ΑΡΙΑΡΤΙΟΝ Poseidon striking with trident; in exergue, ΦΙΛΟ.
208. ↖ 11.79. Stater.

TANAGRA

Obv. Boeotian shield.
Rev. ΤΑ Forepart of horse.
209. ↕ 0.91. Obol.
210. ⤢ 0.88. Obol.

THEBES

Obv. Boeotian shield.
Rev. ΘΕ Amphora.
211. ↘ 11.84. Stater.
212. ↕ 11.85. Stater. *Obv.* on shield, club.

Rev. ΘΕ Infant Herakles strangling serpents.
213. ↕ 11.03. Stater.

Rev. Amphora.
214. ↔ 11.85. Stater. *Rev.* ΗΙΣΜΕ.
215. ↔ 11.92. Stater. *Rev.* ΠΤΟΙ.
216. ↕ 12.15. Stater. *Rev.* ΔΑΜΟΚΛ; above, club.
217. ↕ 5.72. Drachm. *Rev.* type in shallow incuse square; to either side, ΔΙ.

BOEOTIAN FEDERAL COINAGE

Obv. Boeotian shield.
Rev. ΒΟΙ Cantharus; above, club.
218. ↕ 2.69. Triobol.
219. ↕ 2.25. Triobol.

EUBOEA: CHALCIS

Obv. Female head wearing sphendone.
Rev. ΧΑΛ, retrograde. Eagle flying with serpent.

220. ← 3.36. Drachm. *Rev.* above, Ⲏ.

Obv. Female head facing, wearing filleted diadem ornamented with five disks.

221. ← 2.22. Æ. *Rev.* to l., crescent.

HISTIAEA

Obv. Head of maenad wearing vine wreath.
Rev. ΙΣΤΙΑΙΕΩΝ, retrograde on 223. Nymph, holding stylis, seated on stern of galley.

222. ↓ 2.32. Tetrobol. *Rev.* below, ΗΡ.
223. ↙ 2.18. Tetrobol.

ATTICA: ATHENS

References for nos. 225–26 are to C. T. Seltman, *Athens, Its History and Coinage before the Persian Invasion* (Cambridge, Eng., 1924). The dates, however, follow the revised chronology presented by C. M. Kraay in "The Archaic Owls of Athens," *NC* 1956, pp. 43–68.

References for nos. 245–46 are to M. Thompson, *The New Style Silver Coinage of Athens*, ANSNS 10 (New York, 1961).

Obv. Wheel with four spokes.
Rev. Rough quadripartite incuse square.

224. 7.88. Didrachm.

Obv. Head of Athena wearing Attic helmet.
Rev. ΑΘΕ Owl; to l., olive spray.

225. ↖ 16.40. Tetradrachm. Seltman Group M. Late sixth or very early fifth century B.C.
226. ↘ 16.32. Tetradrachm. Seltman Group E. Ca. 500–479 B.C.

Obv. Head of Athena wearing wreathed Attic helmet.
Rev. ΑΘΕ Owl in shallow incuse frame; to l., olive spray; all in shallow incuse circle.

227. ↘ 8.58. Didrachm.

Rev. ΑΘΕ Owl; to l., olive spray and crescent (crescent not present on 236–43); all in shallow incuse square.

228. ↙ 17.13. Tetradrachm.
229. ← 17.10. Tetradrachm.
230. ← 16.98. Tetradrachm.
231. ↙ 17.13. Tetradrachm.
232. ↙ 17.21. Tetradrachm.
233. ← 16.71. Tetradrachm.
234. ← 17.13. Tetradrachm.
235. ↙ 17.10. Tetradrachm.
236. ↖ 4.14. Drachm.
237. ← 4.01. Drachm.
238. ← 1.31. Diobol. *Rev.* double-bodied owl.
239. ↓ 0.74. Obol.
240. ↓ 0.64. Obol.
241. ← 0.63. Obol.
242. ← 0.32. Hemiobol.
243. ↖ 0.31. Hemiobol.

Rev. Ethnic not preserved. Two owls; in center, kalathos; all within olive wreath.

244. → 2.72. Æ.

Obv. Head of Athena Parthenos.
Rev. ΑΘΕ Owl on amphora; all within olive wreath.

245. ↑ 16.40. Tetradrachm. *Rev.* ΕΥΜΗΛΟΣ-ΚΑΛΛΙΦΩΝ-ΗΡΑ; to r., Tyche with cornucopiae and patera; on amphora, Η; below, ΜΕ. Thompson 739a. 140/39 B.C.
246. ↑ 16.39. Tetradrachm. *Rev.* ΔΗΜΗΤΡΙΟΣ-ΑΓΑΘΙΠΠΟΣ-ΑΠ; to r., caps of the Dioscuri; on amphora, Ι; below, ΜΗ. Thompson 899d. 131/0 B.C.

Obv. Head of Athena in Corinthian helmet.
Rev. ΑΘΕ Zeus hurling fulmen; to r., star between crescents.

247. ↑ 7.32. Æ.

MEGARIS: MEGARA

See no. 276 for an Achaean League triobol of Megara.

Obv. Prow; on it, tripod.
Rev. ΜΕΓ Two dolphins.

248. ← 2.40. Æ.

AEGINA

W. L. Brown, "Pheidon's Alleged Aeginetan Coinage," *NC* 1950, pp. 178–204.

Obv. Sea turtle.
Rev. Incuse square divided into five sections.

249. 12.11. Stater. *Obv.* upper edge of shell marked by straight band. Brown Group 2d.
250. 11.98. Stater. *Obv.* lunate countermark. Brown Group 2d.

Obv. Land tortoise.

251. 5.63. Drachm. *Obv.* ΑΙ. *Rev.* Α, Ι, and dolphin in different sections.
252. 4.44. Reduced drachm. *Rev.* double pellet in one section.
253. 2.52. Reduced triobol. *Rev.* as 252.

CORINTHIA: CORINTH

O. E. Ravel, *Les "Poulains" de Corinthe*, (Basel, 1936, and London, 1948).

Obv. ϙ Pegasus flying.
Rev. Swastika-patterned incuse.

254. 8.14. Stater. See Ravel 21-75.

Rev. Head of Athena wearing Corinthian helmet.

255. → 8.20. Stater. *Obv.* ϙ off flan. *Rev.* type in incuse square. See Ravel 170–97.
256. ↗ 8.29. Stater. *Rev.* to r., palmette. See Ravel 341–46 (obv. die of 343–46 ?).
257. ← 8.55. Stater. *Rev.* above, trident. See Ravel 406, 411 (dies of 411 ?).
258. ↑ 8.58. Stater. *Rev.* to l., thymiaterion. See Ravel 580–81, 584 (same obv. die ?).
259. ↖ 8.18. Stater. *Obv.* Pegasus grazing. *Rev.* to r., Zeus standing, holding spear and fulmen. Ravel 699 (this coin).
260. ↓ 8.44. Stater. *Rev.* above, dolphin; to r., cock l. See Ravel 845, 854, 863.
261. ↓ 8.10. Stater. *Rev.* to r., Ε and bow. See Ravel 994, 996.
262. ↓ 8.42. Stater. *Rev.* helmet wreathed; below, ΑΡ; to r., gorgoneion. See Ravel 1009.
263. ↑ 8.30. Stater. *Rev.* helmet wreathed; below, ΑΡ; to r., boar. See Ravel 1017.
264. ↓ 8.49. *Rev.* below, Α; to r., crotalum. See Ravel 1044, described with ΑΛ below. In the ANS collection are coins with the crotalum symbol with Α, and others with ΑΛ; they thus link Ravel's Sixth Series with Α (1035–43) with his Seventh Series with ΑΛ (1044–55).
265. → 8.47. Stater. *Rev.* to l., Δ; to r., Ι and Zeus enthroned, holding fulmen and eagle. See Ravel 1075.

Rev. Head of Aphrodite or Peirene.

266. ↖ 1.72. Drachm. *Rev.* to r., Δ (?).
267. → 2.51. Drachm. *Rev.* to r., ΓΊ.

Rev. Pegasus prancing; below, dolphin; to r., Α.

268. ↑ 0.79. Diobol.

Rev. Trident; to l., Δ (off flan); to r., Ω and covered amphora.

269. ↘ 1.69. Æ.

COLONIES OF CORINTH: LEUCAS

Obv. Λ Pegasus flying.
Rev. Head of Athena wearing Corinthian helmet; all in incuse square.

270. ↙ 8.61. Stater.

THYRRHEIUM

Obv. ΘΥ (obliterated by die break). Pegasus flying.
Rev. ΘΥ Head of Athena wearing Corinthian helmet; to r., Boeotian shield.

271. ↗ 7.94. Stater.

SICYONIA: SICYON

Obv. ΣΙ (ΣΕ on 272). Chimaera.
Rev. Dove flying.

272. → 2.62. Triobol.

273. ↑ 2.60. Triobol.
274. → 2.82. Triobol. *Rev.* to r., NO.

Obv. Laureate head of Apollo.
275. ↖ 0.88. Obol. *Rev.* to l., ΣΙ, retrograde.

ACHAEA: ACHAEAN LEAGUE

M. Thompson, *The Agrinion Hoard*, ANSNNM 159 (New York, 1968).

Obv. Laureate head of Zeus.
Rev. Χ encircled by laurel wreath.
276. ↙ 2.33. Triobol. *Rev.* above, cithara; to l. and r., ΘΟΚΛ. Megara. Thompson 442–48. Ca. 175–168 B.C.
277. ↖ 2.31. Triobol. *Rev.* above, ΘΕ; to l. and r., ΞΕ; below, dolphin. Patras. Thompson 560–63. Ca. 160–150 B.C.
278. ↖ 2.21. Triobol. *Rev.* above, [monogram]; to l. and r., Α[monogram]; below, fulmen. Elis. After 150 B.C. (Thompson, pp. 94–95 and 115).
279. ↙ 2.28. Triobol. *Rev.* to l. and r., ΤΕ. Tegea. Ca. 160–150 B.C. (Thompson, pp. 94 and 115).

PATRAS

See no. 277 for an Achaean League triobol of Patras.

ELIS

See no. 278 for an Achaean League triobol of Elis.

C. T. Seltman, *The Temple Coins of Olympia* (Cambridge, Eng., 1921) (repr. from *Nomisma* 8 [1913], 9 [1914], and 11 [1921]).

Obv. Flying eagle with hare.
Rev. FA Fulmen; all in shallow incuse square.
280. ← 5.44. Drachm. Seltman Group C (p. 35; pl. VIII, 7). Ca. 452–432 B.C.

Obv. Head of Hera wearing stephanus decorated with palmettes.
Rev. FA Fulmen; all encircled by olive wreath.
281. ↘ 10.58. Stater. Seltman Group E^1, 285. Ca. 421–385 B.C.

Obv. Laureate head of Zeus.
Rev. FA Eagle standing; to r., olive leaf.
282. ↙ 2.68. Triobol.

ARGOLIS: ARGOS

Obv. Forepart of wolf.
Rev. Large Α in incuse square.
283. ↗ 2.63. Triobol. *Rev.* above, ΑΡ; below, club.
284. ↑ 2.58. Triobol. *Rev.* letters off flan; below, crescent.
285. ↘ 2.71. Triobol. *Rev.* ΛΥΔΙΑΔΑ; below, boar's head.

ARCADIA: ARCADIAN LEAGUE

R. T. Williams, *The Confederate Coinage of the Arcadians in the Fifth Century B.C.*, ANSNNM 155 (New York, 1965).

Obv. Zeus enthroned, holding sceptre and with eagle flying from his hand.
Rev. ΑΡΚΑ, retrograde. Head of goddess in incuse square.
286. ↗ 2.37. Triobol. Mantinea. Williams 221 *bis* (this coin). Ca. 468–460 B.C.

MEGALOPOLIS

J. A. Dengate, "The Triobols of Megalopolis," *ANSMN* 13 (1967), pp. 57–110.

Obv. Laureate head of Zeus.
Rev. [monogram] Pan seated on rock, holding throwing-stick; on his knee, eagle; to r., Δ over Λ.
287. ↗ 2.41. Triobol. Dengate Group I, Period IIB. Ca. 182–168 B.C.
288. → 2.39. Triobol. As 287.

TEGEA

See no. 279 for an Achaean League triobol of Tegea.

CRETE: CNOSSUS

Obv. Diademed head of Zeus.
Rev. [K]ΝΩ[Σ]Ι[ΩΝ] Square labyrinth.
289. ↖ 1.22. Æ.

AEGEAN ISLANDS: PAROS

Obv. Goat kneeling.
Rev. Quadripartite incuse square.
290. 5.79. Drachm.

THERA (?)

Obv. Two dolphins swimming in opposite directions.
Rev. Incuse square divided into six sections.
291. 12.15. Stater.

PONTUS: AMISUS

Obv. Head of Tyche wearing turreted stephanus.
Rev. Facing owl on shield (off flan); to l., Ⓚ; to r., ΠΑ (monogram).
292. ↙ 4.09. Drachm.

Obv. Head of Athena Parthenos.
Rev. ΑΜΙΣΟΥ Perseus holding harpa and head of Medusa; at his feet, decapitated corpse of Medusa; to l., (monogram) (?).
293. ↑ 19.52. Æ. Reign of Mithradates VI Eupator, 118–63 B.C.

Obv. Aegis with gorgoneion in center.
Rev. ΑΜΙΣΟΥ Nike carrying filleted branch; to l., and r., uncertain monograms.
294. ↗ 7.31. Æ. Reign of Mithradates VI Eupator, 118–63 B.C.

KINGDOM OF THE CIMMERIAN BOSPORUS: SAUROMATES

Obv. ΒΑϹΙΛΕѠϹ ϹΑΥΡΟΜΑΤΟΥ Diademed bust of Sauromates.
Rev. ΜΗ within oak wreath.
295. ↖ 10.80. Æ.

PAPHLAGONIA: SINOPE

Obv. Head of Sinope wearing sphendone.
Rev. ΣΙΝΩ Sea eagle on dolphin; above, ΔΗ.
296. ↗ 6.10. Drachm.

IMITATION OF SINOPE

Obv. Head of Sinope wearing sphendone.
Rev. WIIП Sea eagle on dolphin; to r., L.
297. ↗ 5.73. Drachm.

KINGS OF BITHYNIA: PRUSIAS II

Obv. Head of Prusias wearing winged diadem.
Rev. ΒΑΣΙΛΕΩΣ ΠΡΟΥΣΙΟΥ Herakles standing, holding club and lion's skin; to r., (monogram) (?).
298. ↑ 3.86. Æ.

MYSIA: CYZICUS

H. von Fritze, "Die Elektronprägung von Kyzikos," *Nomisma* 7 (1912), pp. 1–38.

Obv. Hound on tunny.
Rev. Quadripartite incuse square.
299. 2.90. EL hecte. Von Fritze 93. Ca. 550–475 B.C.

PERGAMUM

Obv. Head of Herakles wearing lion's skin headdress.
Rev. ΠΕΡΓΑ Palladium with filleted shield.
300. ↖ 1.22. Diobol.

KINGS OF PERGAMUM

U. Westermark, *Das Bildnis des Philetairos von Pergamon*, Acta Universitatis Stockholmiensis, Studies in Classical Archaeology (Stockholm, 1961).

EUMENES I

Obv. Laureate head of Philetairus.
Rev. ΦΙΛΕΤΑΙΡΟΥ Athena enthroned, holding shield; to l., ivy leaf; on throne, A; to r., bow (off flan).
301. ↑ 16.63. Tetradrachm. See Westermark Group III, V. XXIX.

ATTALUS I

Obv. Laureate head of Philetairus.
Rev. ΦΙΛΕΤΑΙΡΟΥ Athena enthroned, holding shield and spear and crowning the king's name; to outer l., ivy leaf; to inner l., A; to r., bow.

302. ↑ 16.95. Tetradrachm. Westermark Group IVA, V.XLVIII:A.

Obv. Cista mystica with serpent; all in ivy wreath.
Rev. ΠΕ Bow in case between serpents; above, ΔΗ and ΠΡΥ; to r., serpent-staff.

303. ↑ 12.44. Cistophoric tetradrachm.

PITANE

Obv. Head of Zeus Ammon.
Rev. ΠΙΤΑ Pentagram.

304. 3.52. Æ.

TROAS: ABYDUS

Obv. Laureate head of Apollo.
Rev. ΑΒΥ Eagle; to l., tripod; to r., ΛΥΣΑΣ.

305. → 2.57. Hemidrachm.

ALEXANDRIA

Obv. Facing head of Apollo.
Rev. ΑΛΕΞΑΝ Cithara; below, ΜΠ; all in laurel wreath.

306. ↓ 6.95. Æ.

LESBOS

Obv. Two calves' heads facing each other; above, olive tree.
Rev. Incuse square.

307. 11.02. Billon stater.

Obv. Head of ram; below, cock (not preserved).
Rev. Head of Herakles wearing lion's skin headdress; below, club; to l., small square; all in intaglio.

308. ↖ 2.49. EL hecte.

Obv. Head of lion.
Rev. Head of calf, in intaglio.

309. ↖ 2.57. EL hecte.

Obv. Bearded head of satyr wearing fillet.
Rev. Two ram's heads facing each other; above, floral spray; all in incuse square.

310. ↖ 2.48. EL hecte.

Obv. Laureate head of Apollo.
Rev. Female head in linear square.

311. ↖ 2.51. EL hecte.

Obv. Laureate head of Asclepius.
Rev. Forepart of snake in linear square.

312. ↗ 2.52. EL hecte.

Obv. Veiled head of Demeter wearing grain wreath.
Rev. Filleted tripod in linear square.

313. ↑ 2.52. EL hecte.

METHYMNA

Obv. Armored warrior kneeling, holding spear and shield.
Rev. Rider on forepart of horse.

314. ↓ 2.70. Triobol.

UNCERTAIN OF ASIA MINOR

Obv. Raised rough square.
Rev. Rough incuse pattern.

315. 4.30. EL trite.

Obv. Bull's head.
Rev. Rough quadripartite incuse square.

316. 2.32. EL hecte. An attribution to Samos has been proposed: R. Jameson, "Trouvaille de Vourla," *RN* 1911, pp. 60–68.

IONIA: CLAZOMENAE

Obv. Forepart of winged boar.
Rev. Quadripartite incuse square.

317. 0.98. Diobol.

COLOPHON

Obv. Laureate head of Apollo.
Rev. ΚΟΛΟΦΩ Cithara; to r., ΠΟΔΩΡΟΣ.

318. ↑ 3.46. Drachm.

EPHESUS

F. S. Kleiner, *The Early Cistophoric Coinage*, ANSNS 14 (New York, 1977).

Obv. ΕΦ Bee.
Rev. Quadripartite incuse square.

319. 1.41. Diobol.

Rev. Forepart of stag, looking back; to l., palm tree; to r., ΙΠΠΟΔΑΜΑΣ.

320. ↑ 14.79. Tetradrachm.

Rev. Stag kneeling and looking back; to r., bee.

321. ↑ 4.33. Æ.

Obv. Cista mystica with serpent; all in ivy wreath.
Rev. ΕΦΕ Bow in case between serpents; to r., Artemis.

322. ↑ 12.50. Cistophoric tetradrachm. Kleiner Ephesus Series 14, 18-c (this coin). 160–150 B.C.

ERYTHRAE

Obv. Head of Herakles wearing lion's skin headdress.
Rev. ΕΡΥ No type.

323. ↑ 3.33. Æ. *Rev.* ΑΓΑΣΙΚΛΗΣ ΑΝΤΙΠΑΤΡΟΥ.

324. ↑ 3.34. Æ. *Rev.* ΒΑΤΑΚΟΣ ΠΑΡΑΜΟΝΟΥ.

MAGNESIA

Obv. Diademed head of Artemis; at shoulder, animal-headed bow and quiver.
Rev. ΜΑΓΝΗΤΩΝ Apollo, holding fillet, leaning against tripod, which is surmounted by vessel; below, cruciform maeander; to l., ΕΥΦΗΜΟΣ ΠΑΥΣΑΝΙΟΥ; all in laurel wreath.

325. ↑ 14.99. Tetradrachm.

MILETUS

Obv. Laureate head of Apollo.
Rev. ΜΙΛΗΣΙΩΝ Lion standing, looking back; to l., ⋈ and ΣΤΡ; above, star; in exergue, ΣΑΤΥΡΟΣ.

326. ↑ 13.15. Æ.

PHOCAEA

Obv. Laureate female head with hair in saccos; below, small seal (off flan).
Rev. Quadripartite incuse square.

327. 2.55. EL hecte.

SMYRNA

Obv. Head of Cybele wearing turreted crown.
Rev. ΣΜΥΡΝΑΙΩΝ; below, [monogram]; all in oak wreath.

328. ↑ 16.51. Tetradrachm.

Obv. Laureate head of Apollo.
Rev. ΣΜΥΡΝΑΙΩΝ Homer seated, holding scroll; to l., [Α]ΡΙΣΤΟΚΡΑΤ[ΗΣ].

329. ↑ 7.32. Æ.

TEOS

Obv. Griffin.
Rev. Quadripartite incuse square.

330. 11.55. Stater.

IONIA: ISLANDS: CHIOS

J. Mavrogordato, "A Chronological Arrangement of the Coins of Chios," *NC* 1915, pp. 1–52; and "A Chronological Arrangement of the Coins of Chios; Part II," in the same volume, pp. 361–429.

Obv. Sphinx; to l., amphora (331) or grape cluster and amphora (332–33).

331. 7.72. Didrachm. Mavrogordato Period III. Ca. 545–500 B.C.
332. 7.75. Didrachm. Mavrogordato Period V. Ca. 478–431 B.C.
333. 7.82. Didrachm. As 332.

SAMOS

Obv. AVT K ΠΟ· ΛΙΚΙΝ· ΓΑΛΛΙΗΝΟC Laureate bust of Gallienus, wearing paludamentum.
Rev. CAMIΩN Cult-statue of Samian Hera.
334. ↓ 8.44. Æ.

CARIA: CNIDUS

H. A. Cahn, *Knidos. Die Münzen des sechsten und des fünften Jahrhunderts v. Chr.*, AMUGS 4 (Berlin, 1970).

Obv. Forepart of lion.
Rev. Head of Aphrodite in incuse square.
335. ↗ 6.21. Drachm. Cahn Series 3. 490–465 B.C.

HALICARNASSUS

Obv. Head of Poseidon.
Rev. ΑΛΙΚΑΡ Trident adorned with dolphins; to r., uncertain inscription.
336. ↑ 4.72. Æ.

CARIAN ISLANDS: CALYMNA

Obv. Male head wearing crested Attic helmet.
Rev. ΚΑΛΥΜΝΙΟΝ Cithara.
337. ↙ 6.58. Didrachm.

RHODES: CAMIRUS

Obv. Fig leaf.
Rev. Two oblong incuse patterns.
338. 11.99. Stater.

RHODES

Obv. Head of Helios, facing on 339 and 341, and radiate on 340 and 341.
Rev. ΡΟΔΙΟΝ Rose; to l., grape cluster and E; to r., bud.
339. ↑ 6.12. Didrachm. Holed.

Rev. ΡΟ Rose; above, ΑΓΗΣΙΔΑΜΟΣ; to l., helmet; to r., bud.
340. ↑ 2.71. Drachm.

Rev. ΡΟ Open rose; above, branch; below, ear of grain; all in dotted circle.
341. ↓ 4.21. Drachm.

LYDIAN KINGS: BEFORE CROESUS

Obv. Head of lion with nose wart.
Rev. Two incuse squares.
342. 4.69. EL trite.

CROESUS

Obv. Foreparts of lion and bull face to face.
Rev. Two incuse squares.
343. 8.01. AV stater.

PHRYGIA: ACMONEIA

Obv. Head of Cybele wearing turreted crown.
Rev. AKMON[ЄΩN(?)] Artemis standing, holding bow; to r., stag; to l., ΤΙΜΟΘЄΟ[Υ(?)] ΜЄΝЄΛΑ-[ΟΥ(?)].
344. ↑ 4.73. Æ.

APAMEIA

Obv. Laureate head of Zeus.
Rev. ΑΠΑΜΕ[ΩΝ] Cult-statue of Artemis Anaïtis; to l., ΜΗΤΡΟ-ΔΩ[ΡΟΣ] ΔΙΟΤΙΜ[ΟΥ].
345. ↗ 6.50. Æ.

LYCIA: UNCERTAIN DYNAST

Obv. Forepart of boar; on shoulder, [symbol].
Rev. Patterned incuse square.
346. 9.15. Stater.

PAMPHYLIA: ASPENDUS

Obv. Two wrestlers; below, ΑΦ.
Rev. ΕΣΤFΕΔΙΙΥΣ Slinger; to r., triskeles.

347. ↑ 10.34. Stater.

SIDE

See no. 351 for a tetradrachm of Amyntas of Galatia struck at Side.

CILICIA: OLBA

Obv. ΣΕΒΑΣΤΟΣ ΣΕΒΑΣΤΟΥ ΚΑΙ-[ΣΑΡ] Laureate head of Tiberius.
Rev. [ΚΕΝΝΑΤΩΝ ΚΑΙ] ΛΑΛΑΣΣΕΩΝ Fulmen; above and below, ΑΡ-ΧΙΕΡΕΩΣ ΑΙΑΝΤΟΣ ΤΕΥΚΡΟΥ ΤΟΠΑΡΧΟΥ ΕΠΙ ΔΙΟΔΩ and ∢Τ Ε (year 5).

348. ↓ 12.79. Æ.

CYPRUS: PUMIATHON OF CITIUM

Obv. Herakles wearing lion's skin and brandishing club and bow, to r., ankh.
Rev. *Pumiathon* (Phoenician inscription, only partially preserved). Lion attacking stag.

349. ↑ 4.16. AV half stater.

KOINON

Obv. [TI·CL]AVDIVS·CAESAR·AVG·P·M·TR·P[·IMP·] Laureate head of Claudius.
Rev. ΚΟΙΝΟΝ ΚΥΠΡΙΩΝ within laurel wreath.

350. ↑ 9.60. Æ.

GALATIA: AMYNTAS

Obv. Head of Athena wearing crested Corinthian helmet; to l., [monogram].
Rev. ΒΑΣΙΛΕΩΣ ΑΜΥΝΤΟΥ Nike holding filleted sceptre; to l., ΙΒ (year 12).

351. ↑ 15.74. Tetradrachm. Struck at Side.

CAPPADOCIAN KINGS: ARIOBARZANES I

Obv. Diademed head of Ariobarzanes I.
Rev. ΒΑΣΙΛΕΩΣ ΑΡΙΟΒΑΡΖΑΝΟΥ ΦΙΛΟΡΩΜΑΙΟΥ Athena holding Nike and spear; to l., [monogram]; below, traces of ΚΗ (year 28).

352. ↑ 4.14. Drachm. The ANS has five drachms with this monogram, and all are dated ΚΗ. One is from our obverse die, and the tops of its date letters have long serifs extending to the left, similar to the preserved portions of our letters.

SELEUCID KINGS OF SYRIA

E. T. Newell, *The Coinage of the Western Seleucid Mints*, ANSNS 4 (New York, 1941).
E. T. Newell, "The Pre-Imperial Coinage of Roman Antioch," *NC* 1919, pp. 69–113.
E. T. Newell, "The Seleucid Mint of Antioch," *AJN* 51 (1917), pp. 1–151.

ANTIOCHUS I

Obv. Macedonian shield with anchor on boss.
Rev. ΒΑΣΙΛΕΩΣ ΑΝΤΙΟΧΟΥ Elephant; beneath belly, Θ; between hind legs, [monogram].

353. ↖ 4.75. Æ. Newell (*WSM*) 943. Antioch on the Orontes. Ca. 278–268 B.C.

Obv. Diademed head of Antiochus I.
Rev. ΒΑΣΙΛΕΩΣ ΑΝΤΙΟΧΟΥ Apollo seated on omphalos, holding bow and arrow; to l., probable traces of [monogram] (partially off flan); to r., [monogram].

354. ↘ 4.31. Æ. Probably Newell (*WSM*) 961. Antioch on the Orontes. Ca. 268–261 B.C.

ANTIOCHUS I OR II

Obv. Laureate head of Apollo.
Rev. ΒΑΣΙΛΕΩΣ ΑΝΤΙΟΧΟΥ Tripod; below, anchor; to r., Θ (?).

355. ↑ 3.94. Æ. See Newell (*WSM*) 1379–80 (with different reverse letters). Sardes.

ANTIOCHUS III

Obv. Diademed head of Antiochus III.
Rev. ΒΑΣΙΛΕΩΣ ΑΝΤΙΟΧΟΥ Apollo seated on omphalos, holding bow and arrow; to l., uncertain markings.

356. ↙ 3.91. Drachm.

ANTIOCHUS IV

Obv. Bust of Isis wearing grain wreath.
Rev. ΒΑΣΙΛΕΩΣ ΑΝΤΙΟΧΟΥ ΘΕΟΥ ΕΠΙΦΑΝΟΥΣ Eagle on fulmen.

357. ↑ 21.23. Æ. Newell ("Antioch") 60. Antioch on the Orontes. Ca. 168 B.C.

Obv. Diademed and radiate head of Antiochus IV.
Rev. ΑΝΤΙΟΧΕΩΝ ΤΩΝ ΠΡΟΣ ΔΑΦΝΗΙ Zeus standing, holding wreath (off flan); to l. and r., traces of uncertain monograms.

358. ↑ 7.61. Æ. See Newell ("Antioch"), p. 24. Antioch on the Orontes. Ca. 169–167 B.C.

DEMETRIUS I

Obv. Laureate head of Apollo.
Rev. ΒΑΣΙΛΕΩΣ ΔΗΜΗΤΡΙΟΥ Filleted tripod.

359. ↑ 17.04. Æ. Serrated edge. See Newell ("Antioch"), pp. 45–46. Antioch on the Orontes.

ALEXANDER I BALA

Obv. Diademed head of Alexander I Bala.
Rev. ΒΑΣΙΛΕΩΣ ΑΛΕΞΑΝΔΡΟΥ [ΘΕ]ΟΠΑΤΟΡ[ΟΣ ΕΥΕΡΓΕΤΟΥ] Apollo seated on omphalos, holding bow and arrow.

360. ↑ 4.11. Drachm.

ANTIOCHUS VI

Obv. Radiate head of Antiochus VI, wearing ivy wreath.
Rev. ΒΑΣΙΛΕΩΣ ΑΝΤΙΟΧΟΥ ΕΠΙΦΑΝΟΥΣ ΔΙΟΝΥΣΟΥ Elephant holding torch in trunk; above, ΣΤΑ; to r., cornucopiae.

361. ↑ 6.93. Æ. Serrated edge. See Newell ("Antioch"), p. 70. Antioch on the Orontes.

TRYPHON

Obv. Diademed head of Tryphon.
Rev. ΒΑΣΙΛΕΩΣ ΤΡΥΦΩΝΟΣ ΑΥΤΟΚΡΑΤΟΡΟΣ Macedonian helmet with ibex horn, spike, and cheek pieces; to l. (sideways), ΑΣΚ.

362. ↗ 5.55. Æ. See Newell ("Antioch"), pp. 71–73. Antioch on the Orontes.

PHILIP PHILADELPHUS

Obv. Diademed head of Philip.
Rev. ΒΑΣΙΛΕΩΣ ΦΙΛΙΠΠΟΥ ΕΠΙΦΑΝΟΥΣ ΦΙΛΑΔΕΛΦΟΥ Zeus enthroned, holding Nike and sceptre; above, fulmen; all in laurel wreath (not preserved on 364).

363. ↑ 15.14. Tetradrachm. *Rev.* below throne, **Δ**. Antioch on the Orontes. See Newell ("Antioch") 444–50. Ca. 89–83 B.C.

364. ↗ 15.29. Tetradrachm. *Rev.* to l., [monogram]; below throne, **Δ**; in exergue, date (not preserved). Antioch on the Orontes. Posthumous; and 30 B.C. or later, as shown by the form of the throne leg: Newell ("Roman Antioch"), p. 104.

SYRIA: ANTIOCH ON THE ORONTES

See also nos. 358 and 364.

Obv. Head of Tyche of Antioch, wearing stephane.
Rev. ΑΝΤΙΟΧΕΩΝ·ΔΡ (year 104). Laurel branch.

365. ↑ 3.52. Æ. 55/56 A.D. The dates of this and the following three coins are based on the Caesarian Era, calculated from 49/8 B.C.

SYRIA: ANTIOCH ON THE ORONTES (cont.)

Obv. ΑΝΤΙΟΧΕΩΝ Head of Tyche of Antioch, wearing veil and turreted crown.

Rev. Lighted altar, garlanded; below, ЄΤ ЄΚΡ (year 125).

366. ↑ 5.64. Æ. 76/77 A.D.

LAODICEA AD MARE

Obv. ΑΥΤΟΚΡ ΝЄΡ ΤΡΑΙΑΝΟϹ ΑΡΙϹ ΚΑΙϹ ϹЄΒ ΓЄΡ ΔΑΚ Laureate head of Trajan.

Rev. [ΙΟΥΛΙЄѠΝ ΤѠΝ ΚΑΙ] ΛΑΟΔΙΚЄѠΝ ΒΞΡ (year 162). Head of Tyche of Laodicea, wearing veil and turreted crown; to r., Δ.

367. ↑ 9.05. Æ. 113/114 A.D.

Obv. ΑΥΤΟ ΚΑΙ ΤΙ ΑΔΡΙ ΑΝΤѠΝЄΙΝΟϹ ϹЄΒ Laureate head of Antoninus Pius.

Rev. ΙΟΥΛΙЄѠΝ [ΤѠΝ ΚΑΙ ΛΑΟΔΙΚЄѠΝ] Head of Tyche of Laodicea wearing turreted crown and grape cluster; to l., ΚΟ; to r., ΗΠΡ (year 188).

368. ↑ 7.95. Æ. 139/140 A.D.

PHOENICIA: SIDON

Obv. Temple flanked by two columns; in front, altar.

Rev. ΣΙΔΩΝΙΩΝ Europa riding on bull; in exergue, date (off flan).

369. ↑ 6.63. Æ.

KINGS OF PARTHIA

Attributions to kings are those of W. Wroth in the *British Museum Catalogue.* References are to D. Sellwood, *An Introduction to the Coinage of Parthia* (London, 1971). Mint attributions are those of Sellwood; and Sellwood's attributions to rulers are given in parentheses when they differ from Wroth's.

No attempt has been made to reproduce the forms of the Greek letters, which grow increasingly formalized.

MITHRADATES II

Obv. Diademed bust of Mithradates II.

Rev. ΒΑΣΙΛΕΩΣ ΜΕΓΑΛΟΥ ΑΡΣΑΚΟΥ ΕΠΙΦΑΝΟΥΣ Archer seated on omphalos, holding bow.

370. ↑ 4.20. Drachm. Ecbatana (?). Sellwood 24/7.

ORODES I

Obv. Diademed bust of Orodes I; to l., star; to r., crescent.

Rev. ΒΑΣΙΛΕΩΣ ΒΑΣΙΛΕΩΝ ΑΡΣΑΚΟΥ ΕΥΕΡΓΕΤΟΥ ΔΙΚΑΙΟΥ ΕΠΙΦΑΝΟΥΣ ΦΙΛΕΛΛΗΝΟΣ Archer enthroned, holding bow; behind head, Β; below bow, Κ.

371. ↗ 3.68. Drachm. Sellwood 47/9 (Orodes II).

PHRAATES IV

Obv. Diademed bust of Phraates IV.

Rev. ΒΑΣΙΛΕΩΣ ΒΑΣΙΛΕΩΝ ΑΡΣΑΚΟΥ ΕΥΕΡΓΕΤΟΥ ΔΙΚΑΙΟΥ ΕΠΙΦΑΝΟΥΣ ΦΙΛΕΛΛΗΝΟΣ King Phraates enthroned, holding Nike and sceptre; below throne, ΕΠΣ (year 285 of the Seleucid Era); below legend, Γ ΔΑΙΣΙ.

372. ↗ 10.50. Tetradrachm. Seleucia. Sellwood 54/8. 28/27 B.C.

GOTARZES

Obv. Diademed bust of Gotarzes.

Rev. ΒΑΣΙΛΕΩΣ ΒΑΣΙΛΕΩΝ [ΑΡΣΑΚΟΥ ΕΥΕΡΓΕΤΟΥ ΔΙΚ]ΑΙΟΥ ΕΠΙΦΑΝΟΥΣ ΦΙΛΕΛΛΗΝΟΣ Archer enthroned, holding bow; to r., Ѫ.

373. ↑ 3.70. Drachm. Ecbatana(?) Sellwood 65/30 (Gotarzes II).

VARDANES II

Obv. Facing bust of Vardanes II wearing tiara; to either side, a pellet and a star.

Rev. Nude male figure (Zeus?), holding eagle, standing in arched portico.

374. ↗ 0.93. Æ. Sellwood 67/4 (Vonones II).

PERSIAN EMPIRE

The dates are based on E. S. G. Robinson, "The Beginnings of Achaemenid Coinage," *NC* 1958, pp. 187–93.

Obv. King of Persia running, holding bow and spear.

Rev. Oblong incuse.

375. 8.31. AV daric. After 490 B.C.

376. 8.30. AV daric. As 375.

INDO-BACTRIAN KINGS

The arrangement and attributions are those of P. Gardner in the *British Museum Catalogue.* Individual coin references are to M. Mitchiner, *Indo-Greek and Scythian Coinage,* vols. 1–6 (London, 1975–76). Mitchiner's attributions are given in parentheses when they differ from Gardner's.

The inscriptions in Kharosti are translations of the Greek.

EUCRATIDES

Obv. Head of Eucratides wearing crested helmet.

Rev. ΒΑΣΙΛΕΩΣ ΕΥΚΡΑΤΙΔΟΥ Laureate pilei of the Dioscuri surmounted by stars, and two palms; below, [monogram].

377. ↑ 0.62. Obol. Mitchiner, vol. 1, 181a.

APOLLODOTUS I

Obv. ΒΑΣΙΛΕΩΣ ΑΠΟΛΛΟΔΟΤΟΥ ΣΩΤΗΡΟΣ Elephant; below, [monogram].

Rev. Kharosti inscription. Indian bull; below, [monogram].

378. ↑ 2.40. Drachm. Square. Mitchiner, vol. 2, 207b.

MENANDER

Obv. ΒΑΣΙΛΕΩΣ ΣΩΤΗΡΟΣ ΜΕΝΑΝΔΡΟΥ Diademed bust of Menander; wearing aegis and brandishing spear on 380.

Rev. Kharosti inscription. Athena holding aegis and brandishing fulmen.

379. ↑ 2.43. Drachm. *Rev.* to l., [monogram]. Mitchiner, vol. 2, 215o.

380. ↑ 2.41. Drachm. *Rev.* to l., [monogram]. Mitchiner, vol. 2, 220c.

ZOILUS

Obv. ΒΑΣΙΛΕΩΣ ΣΩΤΗΡΟΣ ΖΩΙΛΟΥ Diademed bust of Zoilus.

Rev. Kharosti inscription. Athena holding aegis and brandishing fulmen; to r., [monogram].

381. ↑ 2.38. Drachm. Mitchiner, vol. 3, 459n (Zoilus II).

ANTIMACHUS II

Obv. ΒΑΣΙΛΕΩΣ ΝΙΚΗΦΟΡΟΥ ΑΝΤΙΜΑΧΟΥ Nike carrying palm and fillet; to l., [monogram].

Rev. Kharosti inscription. Antimachus, wearing kausia and diadem, on horseback.

382. ↖ 2.30. Drachm. Mitchiner, vol. 1, 135c (Antimachus).

HERMAEUS

Obv. ΒΑΣΙΛΕΩΣ ΣΩΤΗΡΟΣ ΕΡΜΑΙΟΥ. Diademed bust of Hermaeus.

Rev. Kharosti inscription. Zeus enthroned, holding Nike and sceptre; to l., [monogram]; to r., [monogram].

383. ↗ 8.43. Æ. Mitchiner, vol. 3, 421b.

MAUES

Obv. Head of elephant wearing bell around neck.

Rev. ΒΑΣΙΛΕΩΣ ΜΑΥΟΥ Caduceus; to l., [monogram].

384. ↑ 9.02. Æ. Mitchiner, vol. 5, 707a.

AZES

Obv. ΒΑΣΙΛΕΩΣ [ΒΑΣΙΛΕΩΝ ΜΕΓΑΛΟΥ] ΑΖΟΥ Azes, diademed and holding whip, on horseback; to r., uncertain Kharosti letter.
Rev. Kharosti inscription. Athena holding shield and lance; to l., [monogram]; to r., [monogram].

385. ↑ 2.12. Drachm. Mitchiner, vol. 6, 827a (Azes II).

EGYPT: PTOLEMAIC KINGS

J. N. Svoronos, *Ta Nomismata tou kratous ton Ptolemaion* (Athens, 1904 and 1908). Attributions are those of Svoronos.

PTOLEMY I

Obv. Head of Alexander wearing elephant's skin headdress and aegis; on aegis, small Δ.
Rev. ΑΛΕΞΑΝΔΡΟΥ Athena Promachus; to r., eagle on fulmen and ΓΗ.

386. ↑ 15.63. Tetradrachm. Svoronos 108.

Obv. Diademed head of Ptolemy I; to l., small Δ.
Rev. ΒΑΣΙΛΕΩΣ ΠΤΟΛΕΜΑΙΟΥ Eagle on fulmen.

387. ↑ 14.27. Tetradrachm. *Rev.* to l., Ρ and [monogram]. Svoronos 255.

Obv. Laureate head of Zeus.

388. ↑ 14.12. Æ. *Rev.* to l., Α and Φ. Svoronos 287.

PTOLEMY II

Obv. Diademed head of Ptolemy I, wearing aegis.
Rev. ΒΑΣΙΛΕΩΣ ΠΤΟΛΕΜΑΙΟΥ Eagle on fulmen; head turned back on 392–93.

389. 14.23. Tetradrachm. *Rev.* to l., [monogram] and shield blazoned with fulmen; to r., [monogram]. Svoronos 555.

Obv. Laureate head of Zeus.

390. ↑ 16.97. Æ. *Rev.* to l., shield blazoned with fulmen. Svoronos 610.

391. ↑ 16.72. Æ. As 390.

Obv. Diademed head of Zeus Ammon.

392. ↑ 48.32. Æ. *Rev.* to upper r., filleted cornucopiae; between eagle's legs, Ε. Svoronos 974.

Obv. Head of Alexander wearing elephant's skin headdress.

393. ↑ 11.41. *Rev.* as 392. Svoronos 976.

PTOLEMY VI

Obv. Head of Isis wearing grain wreath.
Rev. ΒΑΣΙΛΕΩΣ ΠΤΟΛΕΜΑΙΟΥ Eagle on fulmen; to l., [monogram] (?).

394. ↑ 15.29. Æ. Probably Svoronos 1384 (with monogram as given).

PTOLEMY VIII

Obv. Diademed bust of Ptolemy I, wearing aegis.
Rev. ΒΑΣΙΛΕΩΣ ΠΤΟΛΕΜΑΙΟΥ Eagle on fulmen.

395. ↖ 13.10. Tetradrachm. Svoronos 1489.

Obv. Head of Alexandria wearing elephant's skin headdress.

396. ↖ 13.80. Æ. Svoronos 1493.

Obv. Horned head of Arsinoe II, wearing diadem and veil; behind, sceptre; to l., Κ (year 20).
Rev. ΑΡΣΙΝΟΗΣ ΦΙΛΑΔΕΛΦΟΥ Double cornucopiae with fillet.

397. ↑ 27.42. Ꜷ octadrachm. Svoronos 1499.

PTOLEMY XIII

Obv. Diademed head of Ptolemy I.
Rev. ΒΑΣΙΛΕΩΣ ΠΤΟΛΕΜΑΙΟΥ Eagle on fulmen; behind to r., branch; to l., headdress of Isis; to r., ΠΑ.

398. ↑ 14.19. Tetradrachm. *Rev.* to l., LΚΖ (year 27). Svoronos 1836.

399. ↑ 14.61. Tetradrachm. *Rev.* to l., LΚΘ (year 29). Svoronos 1839.

CLEOPATRA VII AND ANTONY

Obv. CLEOPATRAE · REGINAE · REGUM · FILIORUM · REGUM Diademed bust of Cleopatra; to r., prow.

Rev. ANTONI · ARMENIA · DEVICTA Head of Antony; to l., Armenian tiara.

400. ↑ 3.40. Denarius. Svoronos 1906.

EGYPT UNDER THE ROMANS

G. Dattari, *Numi Augg. Alexandrini* (Cairo, 1901).

J. G. Milne, *Catalogue of Alexandrian Coins* (Oxford, 1933), repr. with supplement by C. M. Kraay (Oxford, 1971).

The arrangement and denominations are Milne's.

CLAUDIUS

Obv. TI ΚΛΑΥ ΚΑΙCΕΒΑC ΓΕΡΜΑ Laureate bust of Claudius.

Rev. ΑΥΤΟ ΚΡΑ Bull; below, LB (year 2).

401. ↑ 6.90. Æ diobol. *Obv.* to r., star. Dattari 172. Milne 69–70.

Rev. ΑΥΤΟ ΚΡΑ Winged caduceus and ears of grain tied together.

402. ↗ 6.61. Æ diobol. *Obv.* to r., LIA (year 11). Dattari 141. Milne 119.

NERO

Obv. ΝΕΡΩ ΚΛΑΥ ΚΑΙΣΣΕΒ ΓΕΡ (403–4) or ΝΕΡΩ ΚΛΑΥ ΚΑΙΣΣΕΒ ΓΕΡΑΥ (405–6). Radiate bust of Nero wearing aegis.

Rev. ΑΥΤΟ ΚΡΑ Bust of Alexandria wearing elephant's skin headdress; to r., LIB (year 12).

403. ↑ 12.60. Billon tetradrachm. Dattari 204. Milne 238–39.

Rev. ΑΥΤΟ ΚΡΑ Bust of Roma wearing crested helmet and cuirass; to r., LIΓ (year 13).

404. ↑ 12.82. Billon tetradrachm. Dattari 246. Milne 249–50.

Rev. ΘΕΟΣΣΕΒΑΣΤΟΣ Radiate head of Augustus.

405. ↑ 12.90. Billon tetradrachm. *Obv.* to l., LIΓ (year 13). Dattari 184. Milne 251–55.

Rev. ΤΙΒΕΡΙΟΣ ΚΑΙΣΑΡ Laureate head of Tiberius.

406. ↑ 13.10. Billon tetradrachm. *Obv.* to l., LIΓ (year 13). Dattari 185. Milne 256.

HADRIAN

Obv. ΑVΤ ΚΑΙ ΤΡΑΙ ΑΔΡΙΑ CΕΒ (407), ΑVΤ ΚΑΙC ΤΡΑΙ ΑΔΡΙΑ CΕΒ (408) or ΑVΤ ΚΑΙC ΤΡΑΙΑΝ ΑΔΡΙΑΝΟC CΕΒ (409–10). Laureate bust of Hadrian wearing cloak and cuirass (407–9) or laureate head of Hadrian (410).

Rev. Nilus seated on rocks, holding reed and cornucopiae; on rocks, crocodile; to l., LIϚ (year 16).

407. ↑ 26.20. Æ drachm. Dattari 1794–95. Milne 1329–33.

Rev. Nilus reclining, holding reed and cornucopiae; beside him, crocodile; to l., LIZ (year 17).

408. ↑ 13.30. Billon tetradrachm. Dattari 1434. Milne 1351-52.

Rev. Serpent Agathodaemon on l., crowned with skhent and enfolding caduceus in coils, facing serpent Uraeus on r., crowned with horns and disk and enfolding sistrum; in field, traces of LIH (year 18).

409. ↑ 16.52. Æ drachm. Dattari 1991. Milne 1424.

Rev. Bust of Sarapis wearing taenia and modius; to l., and r., LΕΝΝΕΑΚ · Δ (year 19).

410. ↗ 13.05. Billon tetradrachm. Dattari 1465 (obverse legend slightly shorter). Milne 1446.

ANTONINUS PIUS

Obv. MAVPHΛΙΟCΚΑΙCΑΡ Bust of Marcus Aurelius wearing cloak.

Rev. Tyche standing, wearing modius and holding rudder and cornucopiae; to l., LΙϚ (year 16 of Antoninus Pius).

411. ↑ 15.01. Billon tetradrachm. Dattari 3179. Milne 2183.

COMMODUS

Obv. ΜΑ ΚΟΜΑΝ ΤϢCEBEVCEB Laureate head of Commodus.

Rev. Dikaiosyne seated, holding scales and sceptre; to l., LΚΘ (year 29 of Marcus Aurelius).

412. ↑ 11.31. Billon tetradrachm. Dattari 3863. Milne 2679.

GORDIAN III

Obv. ΑΚΜΑΝ Γ ΟΡΔΙΑΝΟCEVCE Laureate bust of Gordian wearing cloak and cuirass.

Rev. Eagle standing with wings open, holding wreath in beak; in field, LΔ (year 4).

413. ↑ 13.57. Billon tetradrachm. Dattari 4808. Milne 3398.

PHILIP I

Obv. ΑΚΜΙΟVΦΙΛΙΠΠΟCEVCEB Laureate bust of Philip wearing cuirass.

Rev. Tyche standing, wearing modius and holding rudder and cornucopiae; to l., LB (year 2).

414. ↑ 12.04. Billon tetradrachm. Dattari 4920. Milne 3546–47.

GALLIENUS

Obv. AVTKΠΛΙ ΚΓΑΛΛΙΗΝΟCCEB (415, 417), or ΚΟΡΝΗΛΙΑCΑΛϢΝΕΙΝΑCEB (416). Laureate bust of Gallienus wearing cuirass (415, 417), or draped bust of Salonina wearing stephane (416).

Rev. Athena standing, holding spear and shield; to r., palm; to l., LΙΒ (year 12).

415. ↑ 10.25. Billon tetradrachm. Dattari 5228 (without mention of palm). Milne 4098.

Rev. Dikaiosyne standing, holding scales and cornucopiae; to r., palm; to l., LΙΓ (year 13).

416. ↑ 9.20. Billon tetradrachm. Dattari 5328. Milne 4113.

Rev. Bust of Selene wearing chiton and peplos; to r., large crescent; to l., LΙΔ (year 14).

417. ↑ 10.57. Billon tetradrachm. Dattari 5264. Milne 4125.

CLAUDIUS II

Obv. AVTKΚΛΑVΔΙΟCCEB Laureate bust of Claudius II wearing cloak and cuirass.

Rev. Nike inscribing shield placed on column; on shield, LA (year 1).

418. ↑ 8.75. Billon tetradrachm. Dattari 5404. Milne 4199.

Rev. Poseidon standing with foot on dolphin, and holding sword and trident; in field, LB (year 2).

419. ↑ 9.22. Billon tetradrachm. Dattari 5407. Milne 4252-53.

AURELIAN

Obv. AVTKΛΔΑVΡΗΛΙΑΝΟCCEB Laureate bust of Aurelian wearing cloak and cuirass.

Rev. Eagle, with wings open and holding wreath in beak, standing between vexilla; above, LΔ (year 4).

420. ↑ 10.74. Billon tetradrachm. Dattari 5494 (with slightly shorter inscription). Milne 4391–92.

DIOCLETIAN

Obv. ΔΙΟΚΛΗΤΙΑΝΟCCЄΒ Laureate bust of Diocletian.
Rev. Zeus standing, holding patera and sceptre; to l., eagle; in field, LZ (year 7).

421. ↑ 7.62. Billon tetradrachm. Dattari 5776. Milne 4946–66.

CYRENAICA: CYRENE

Obv. ΚΥΡΑΝΑΙΟΝ Nike driving quadriga.
Rev. Zeus Ammon, holding patera and sceptre, sacrificing before thymiaterion; to r., ΠΟΛΙΑΝΘΕΥΣ.

422. ↑ 8.39. AV stater.

Obv. Running horse.
Rev. Wheel with six spokes and hub.

423. 7.51. Æ.

Obv. Head of Carneius.
Rev. ΚΥΡΑ Silphium plant; above, Δ and star.

424. ↘ 7.33. Didrachm.

Obv. Diademed head of Zeus Ammon.
Rev. ΚΟΙΝΟΝ Silphium plant.

425. ↑ 8.55. Æ.

SYRTICA: OEA

Obv. Bust of Livia; to l., trace of grain ear.
Rev. WY'T (Punic legend). Bust of Athena wearing crested Corinthian helmet.

426. ← 6.95. Æ.

ZEUGITANA: CARTHAGE

G. K. Jenkins and R. B. Lewis, *Carthaginian Gold and Electrum Coins* (London, 1963).

E. S. G. Robinson, "Carthaginian and Other South Italian Coinages of the Second Punic War," *NC* 1964, pp. 37–64.

Obv. Palm tree.
Rev. Horse's head.

427. ↘ 7.40. Æ. Sicilian mint.

Obv. Head of Herakles wearing lion's skin headdress.
Rev. MḤSBM (Punic legend). Horse's head; to r., palm tree.

428. ↓ 16.93. Tetradrachm. Sicilian mint. Jenkins-Lewis, p. 22, and p. 129, 42. Late fourth century B.C.

Obv. Head of Tanit wearing grain wreath.
Rev. Horse; behind, palm tree.

429. ↓ 2.61. Æ. Sicilian mint (?). Jenkins-Lewis, p. 132, 1; see pl. 26, 11–12. Late fourth century B.C.

430. ↑ 2.83. Æ. *Obv.* to r., pellet. *Rev.* to r., three pellets above one pellet. Sicilian mint (?). Jenkins-Lewis, p. 133, 13; pl. 26, 12. Late fourth century B.C.

Rev. Horse's head; to r., Punic letter T.

431. ↗ 4.73. Æ. *Obv.* to r., Punic letter B. Sardinia. Jenkins-Lewis, p. 134, Class B; pl. 26, 13. Third century B.C.

Rev. Horse; behind, palm tree.

432. ↑ 11.25. Billon double shekel. Carthage. Jenkins-Lewis, pl. 27, 8. Ca. 240-230 B.C.

Rev. Horse walking, looking back; below, Punic letter K.

433. ↑ 8.81. Æ. Carthage (?). Jenkins-Lewis, pl. 28, 10. Ca. 220–200 B.C.

Rev. Horse; above, sun-disk; below, Punic letter ʿ.

434. ↖ 3.70. Half shekel. Italian mint (?). Robinson, p. 45, 4; see Jenkins-Lewis pl. 28, 3. Ca. 220–210 B.C. The reverse symbol is usually described as flanked by uraei, but the presence of the uraei is questionable.

ISLANDS BETWEEN AFRICA AND SICILY: MELITA

Obv. Veiled female head.

Rev. Mummy of Osiris, holding flail and sceptre, standing between Isis and Nephthys, each with wings folded in front and holding palm branch and uncertain other object.

435. ↙ 10.95. Æ.

NUMIDIAN KINGS: MICIPSA (?)

Obv. Laureate bearded head.

Rev. Horse galloping; below, pellet.

436. ↑ 12.10. Æ.

MAURETANIAN KINGS: JUBA II AND CLEOPATRA SELENE

Obv. REX IVBA Diademed head of Juba II.

Rev. BACIΛICCA ΚΛΕΟΠΑΤΡΑ Star and crescent.

437. ↖ 3.12. Denarius.

PLATES

Plate 1

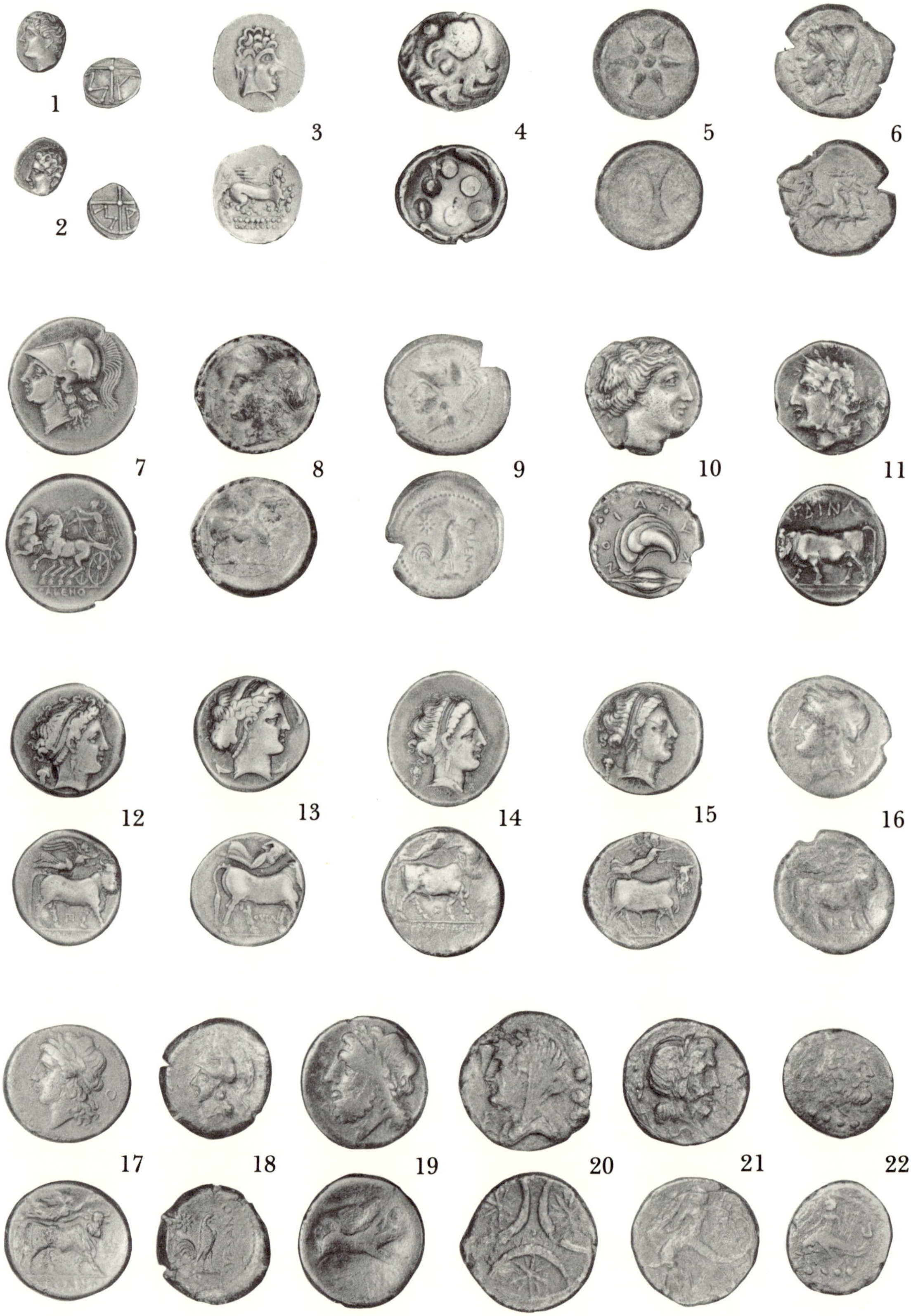

THE JOHN MAX WULFING COLLECTION

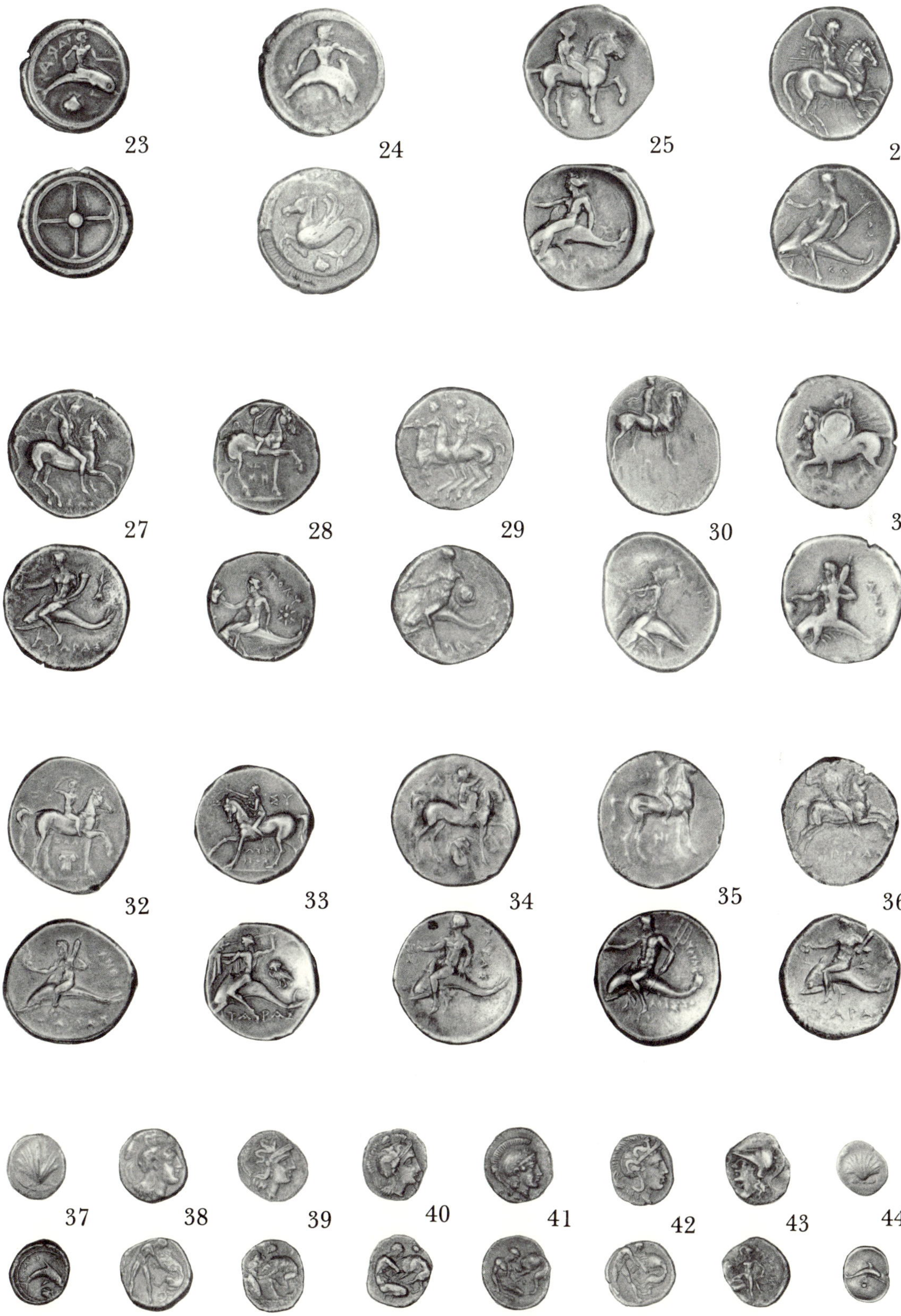

23 24 25 26

27 28 29 30 31

32 33 34 35 36

37 38 39 40 41 42 43 44

THE JOHN MAX WULFING COLLECTION

Plate 3

45 46 47 48 49

50 51 52 53 54

55 56 57 58 59 60

THE JOHN MAX WULFING COLLECTION

61 62 63 64 65

66 67 68 69 70

71 72

73 74 75 76 77 78

THE JOHN MAX WULFING COLLECTION

Plate 5

79 80 81 82 83 84

85 86

87 88 89 90 91 92

93 94 95 96 97

THE JOHN MAX WULFING COLLECTION

98

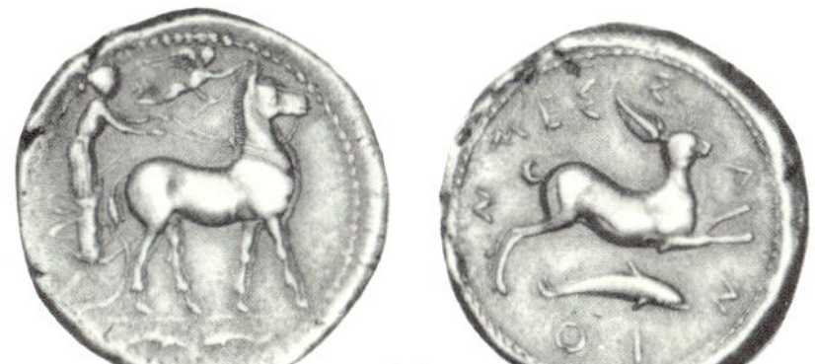

99

100 101 102 103 104 105

106 107 108 109 110

111

112

113

THE JOHN MAX WULFING COLLECTION

Plate 7

114

115

116

117

118

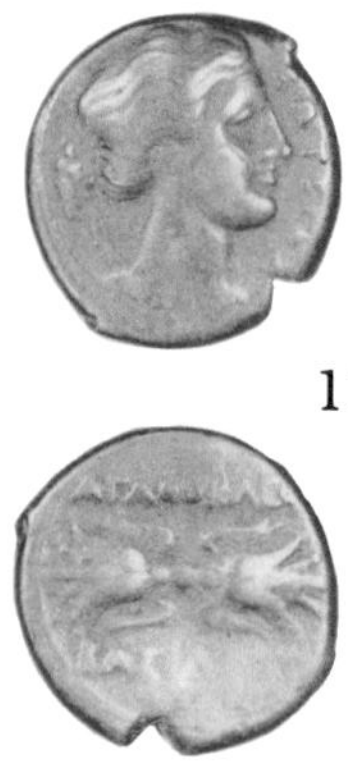
119

120

121

122

123

124

125

126

127

128

129

THE JOHN MAX WULFING COLLECTION

130

131

132

133

134
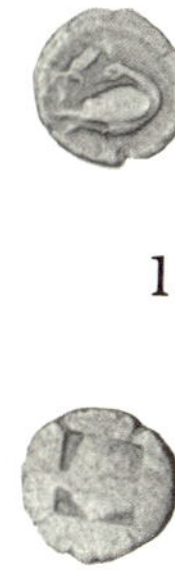
135

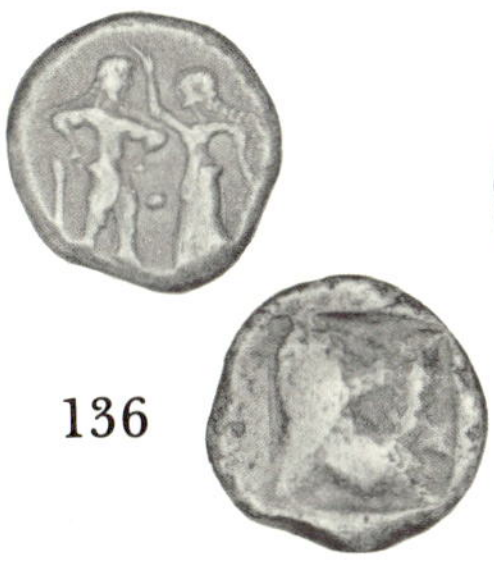
136

137
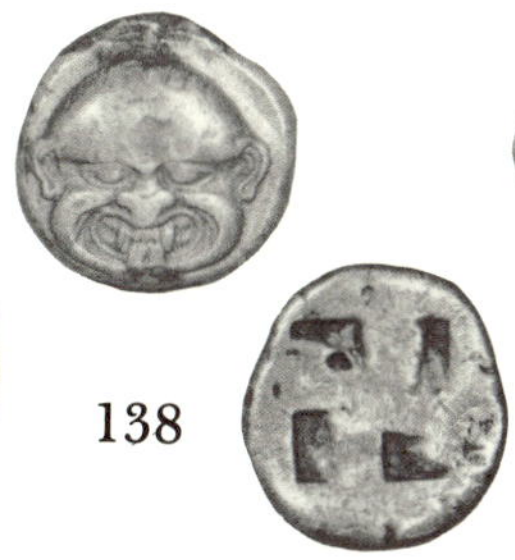
138
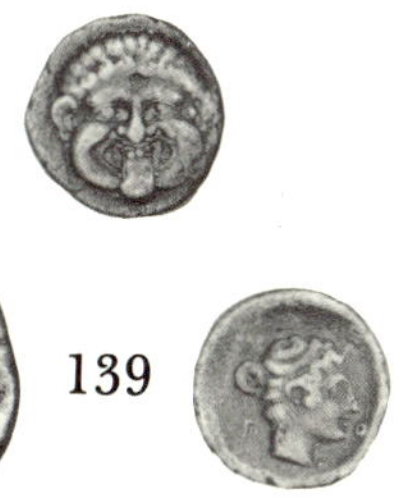
139

140

141

142

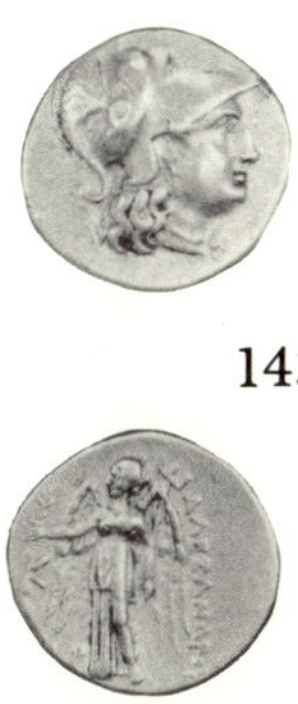
143

144

145

146

147

THE JOHN MAX WULFING COLLECTION

Plate 9

148

149

150

151

152

153

154

155

156

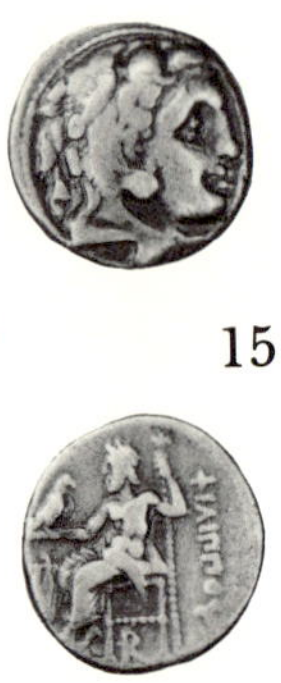
157

158

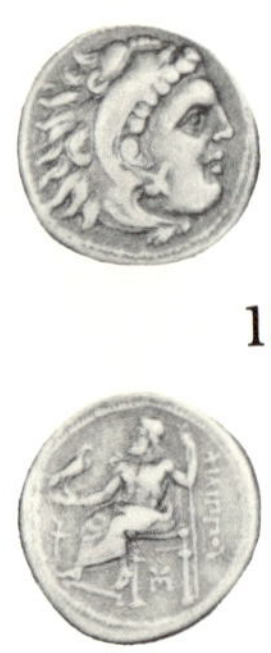
159

160

161

162

163

164

165

166

167

168

169

170

171

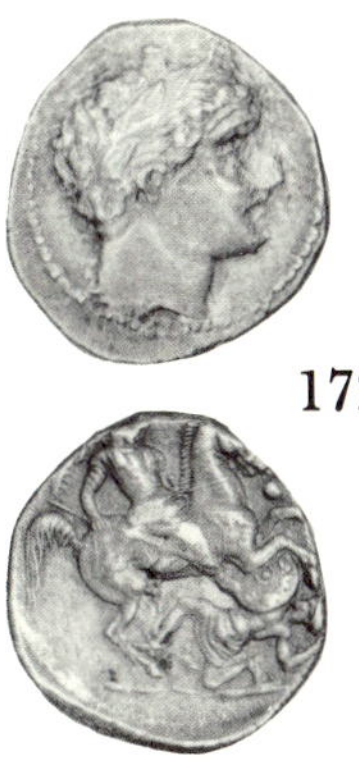
172

173

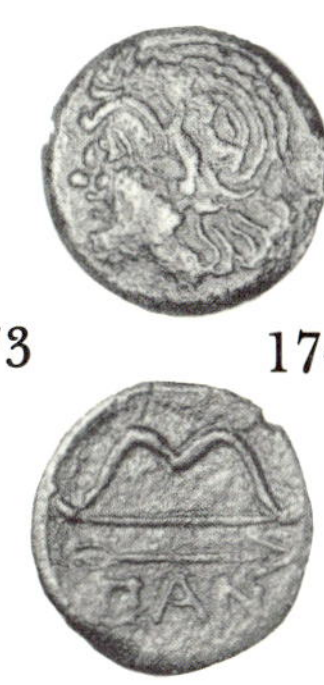
174

175

176

177

178

179

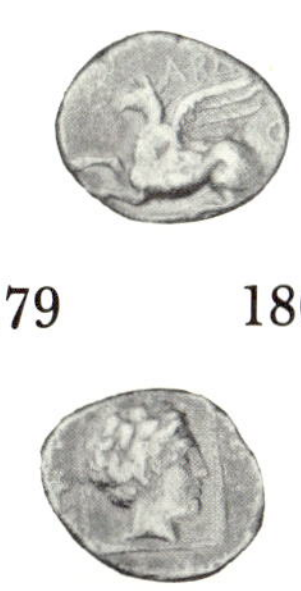
180

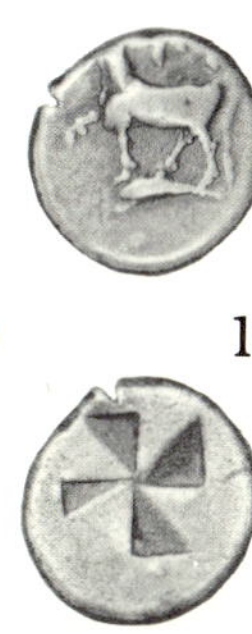
181

182

THE JOHN MAX WULFING COLLECTION

Plate 11

183

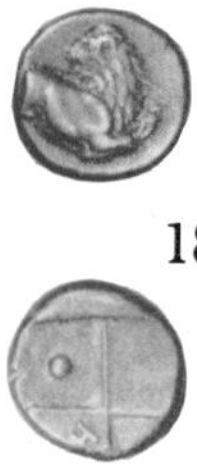
184

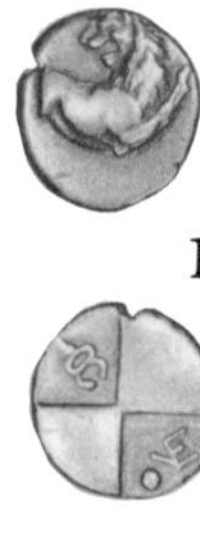
185

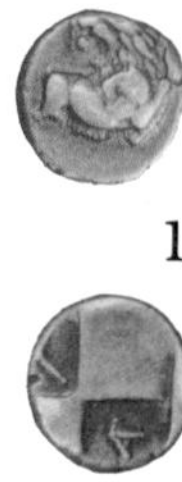
186

187

188

189

190

191

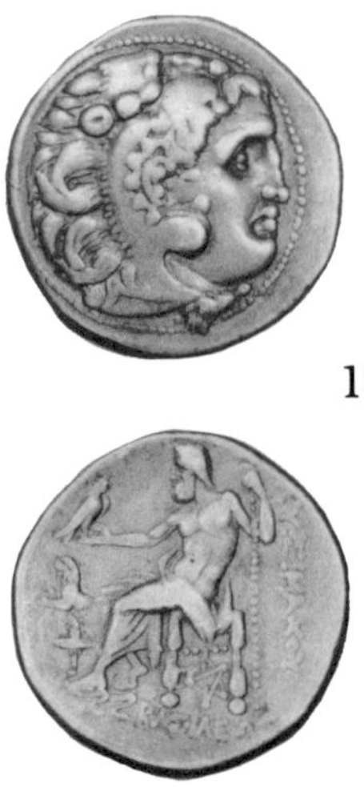
192

193

194

195

196

197

198

199

200

201

THE JOHN MAX WULFING COLLECTION

202 203 204 205 206 207

208 209 210 211 212 213

214 215 216 217 218 219

220 221 222 223

THE JOHN MAX WULFING COLLECTION

Plate 13

224 225 226 227 228 229

230 231 232 233 234 235

236 237 238 239 240 241 242 243 244

245 246 247

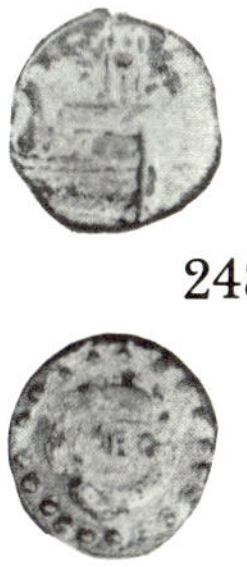
248
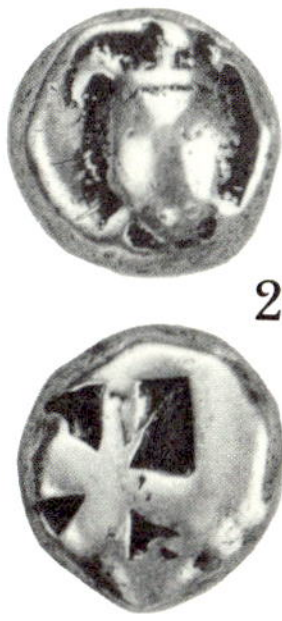
249
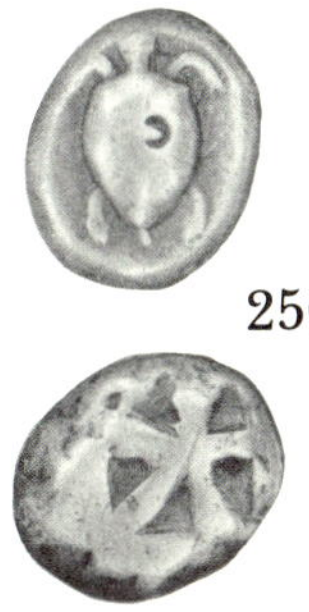
250
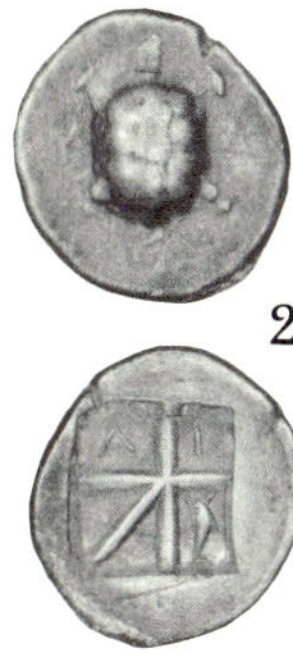
251
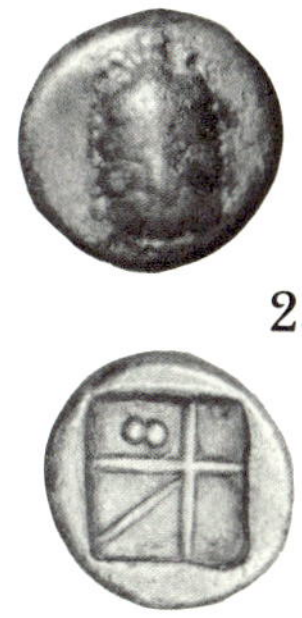
252
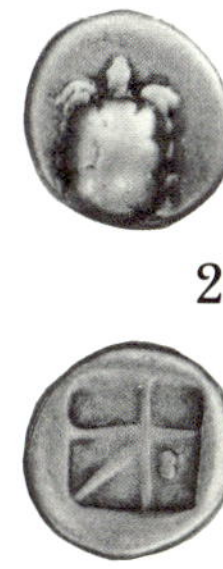
253

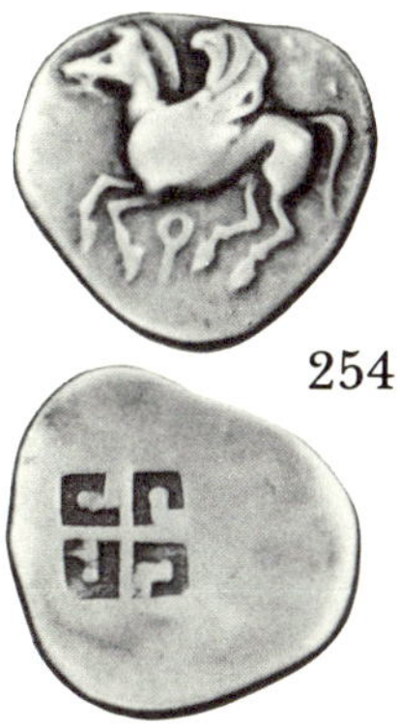
254
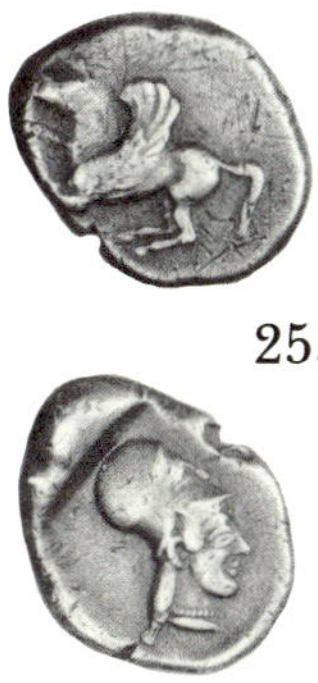
255
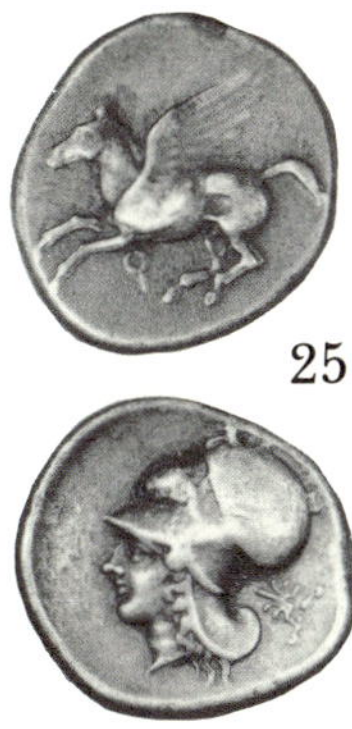
256
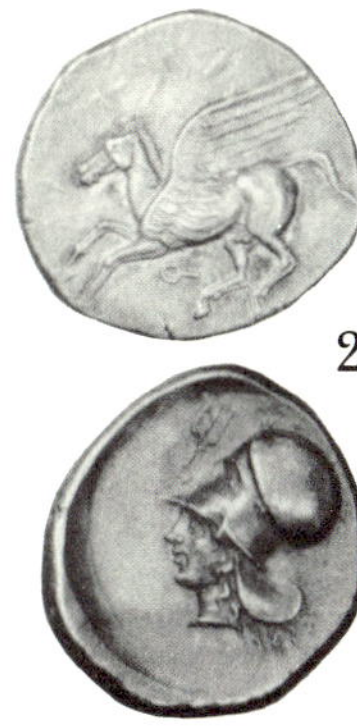
257

258

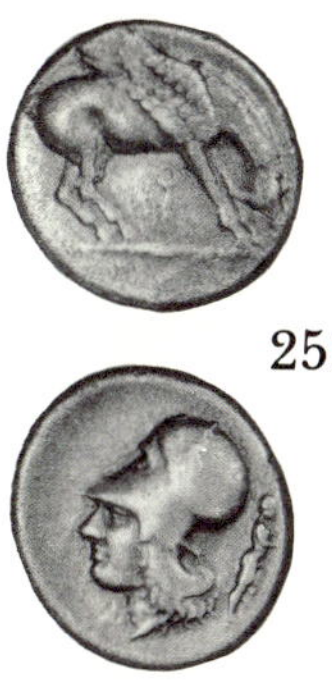
259
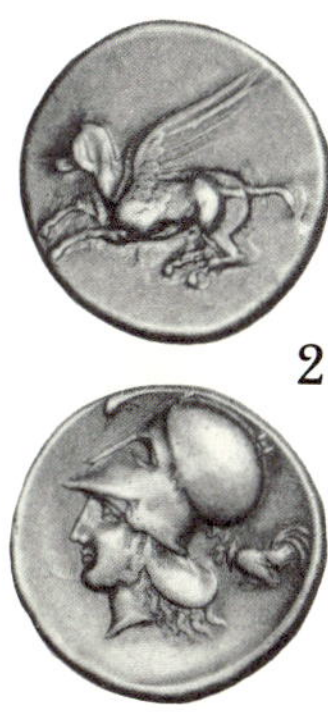
260
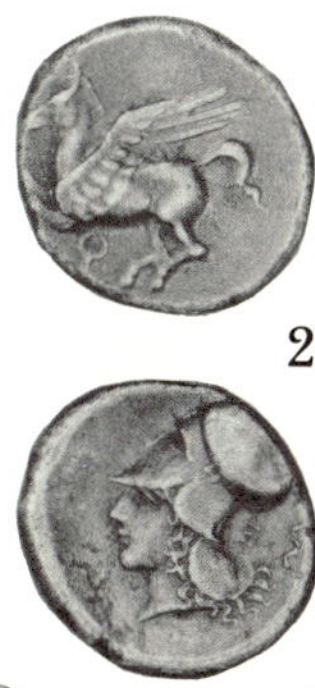
261
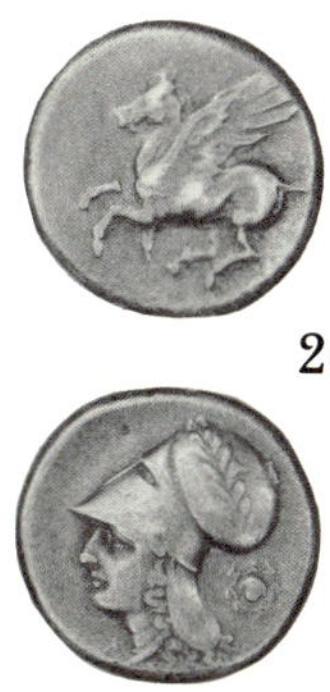
262
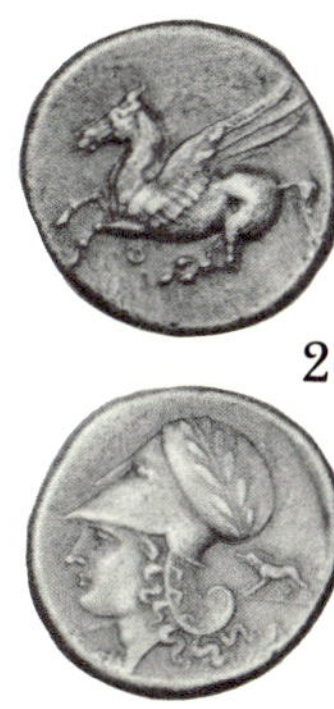
263

266

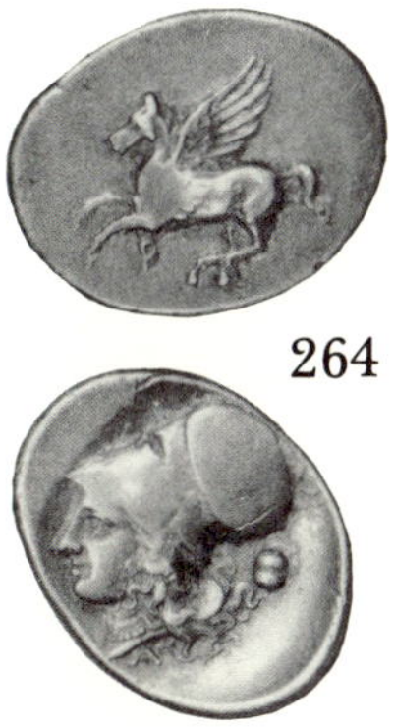
264
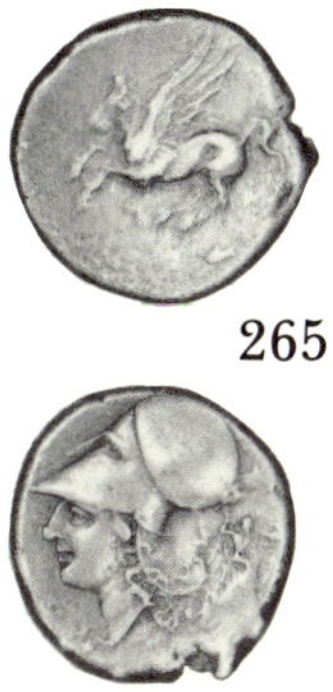
265

267

268

269

270

271

272 273 274 275 276 277 278 279

280 281 282 283 284 285

286 287 288 289 290 291

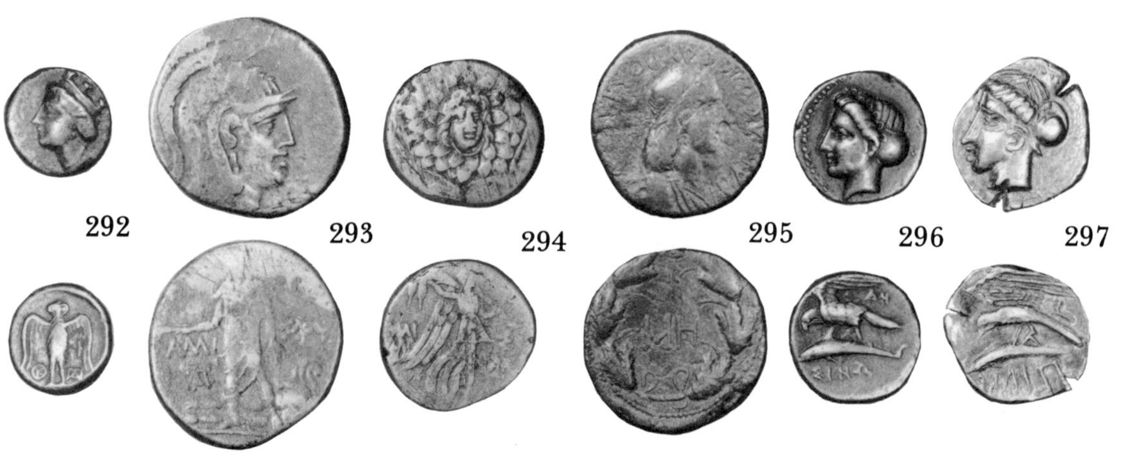

292 293 294 295 296 297

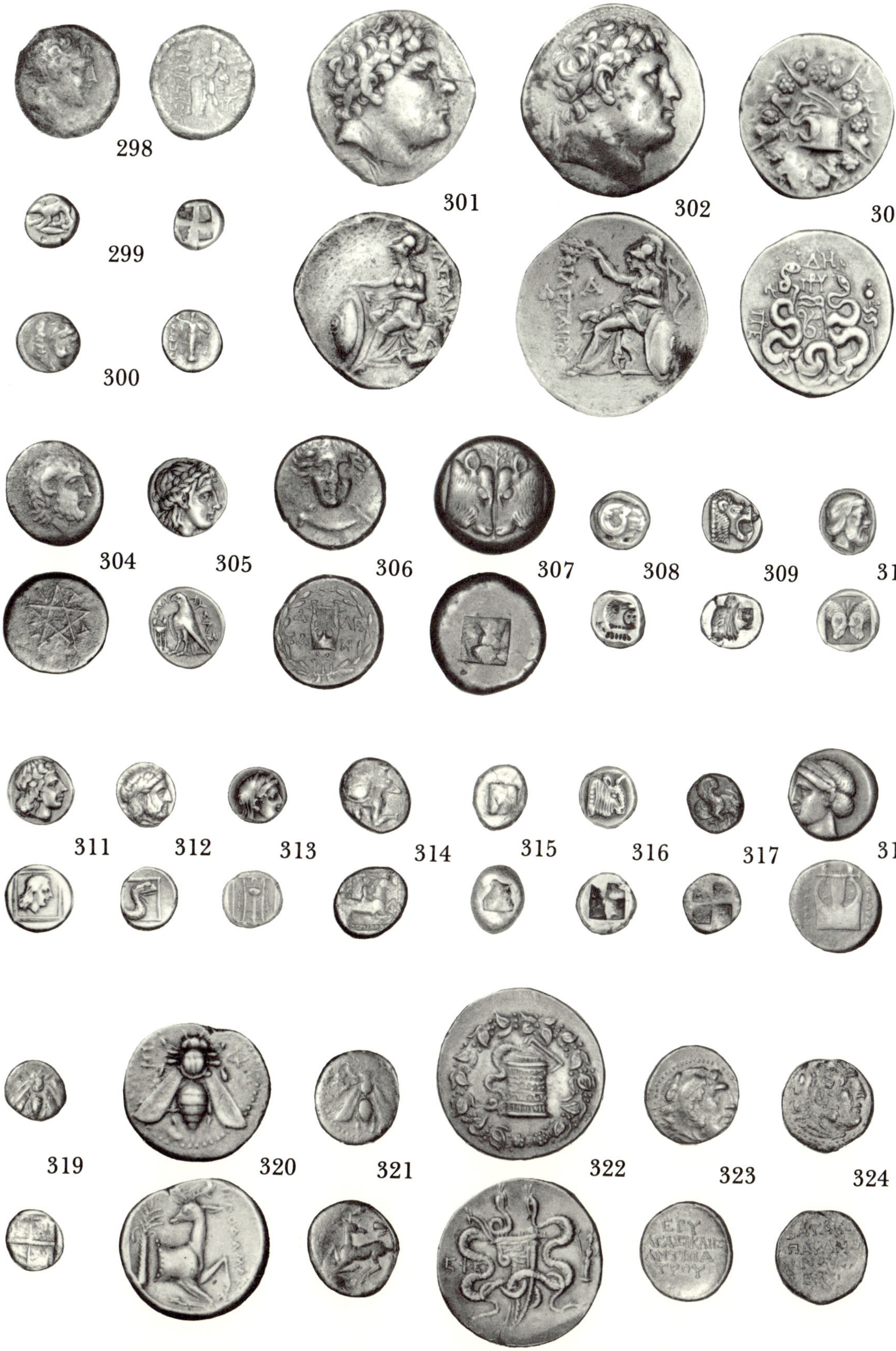

298 299 300 301 302 303

304 305 306 307 308 309 310

311 312 313 314 315 316 317 318

319 320 321 322 323 324

THE JOHN MAX WULFING COLLECTION

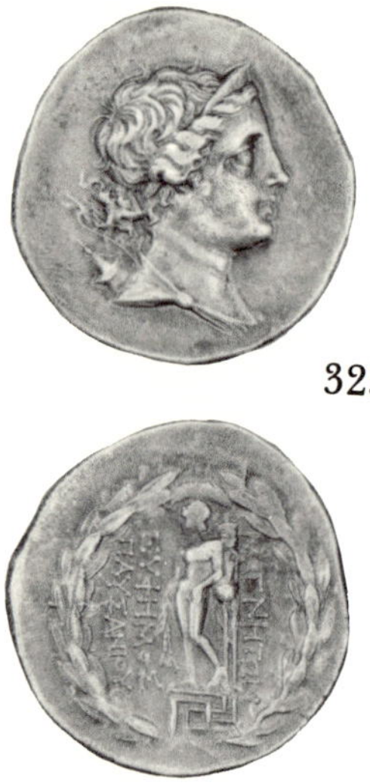

325

326

328

327

329

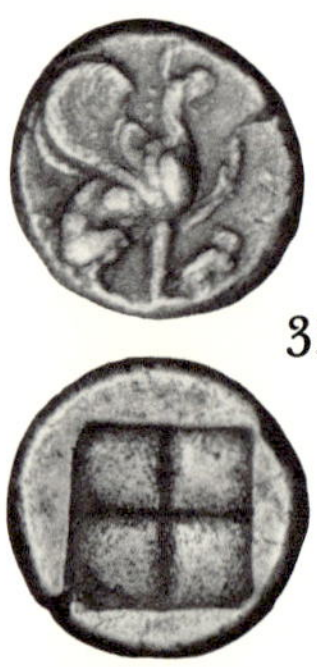

330

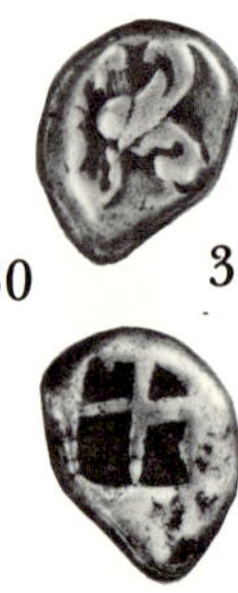

331

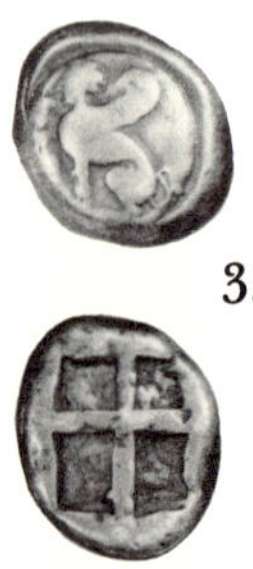

332

333

334

335

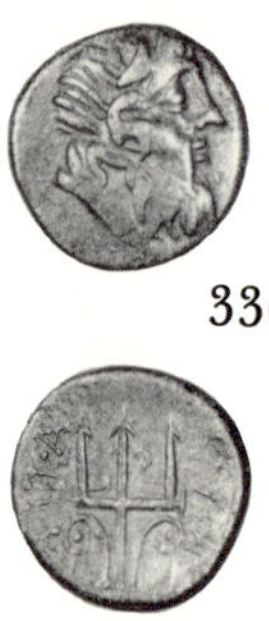

336

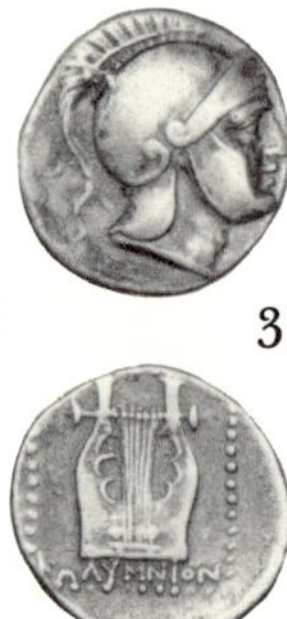

337

338

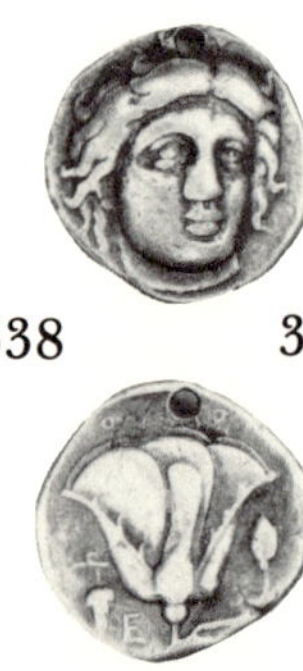

339

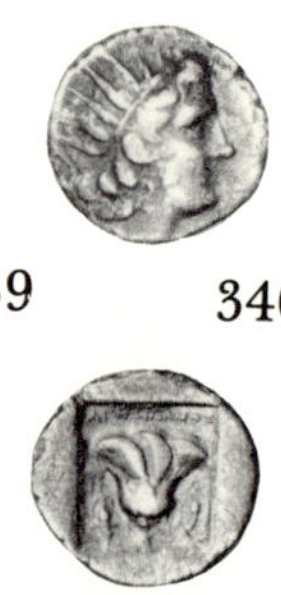

340

341

342

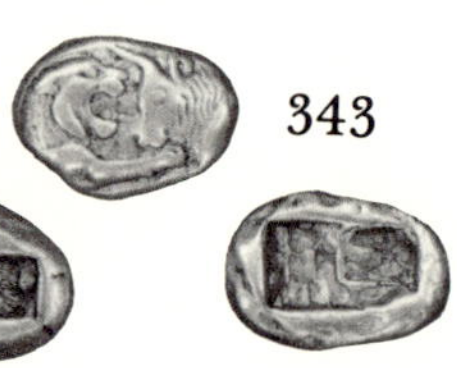

343

344

345

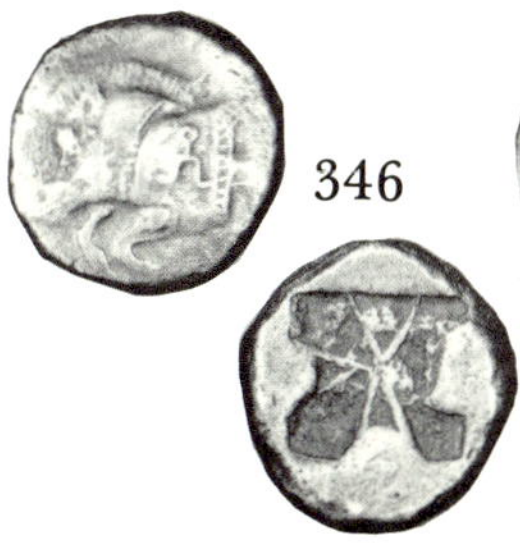
346

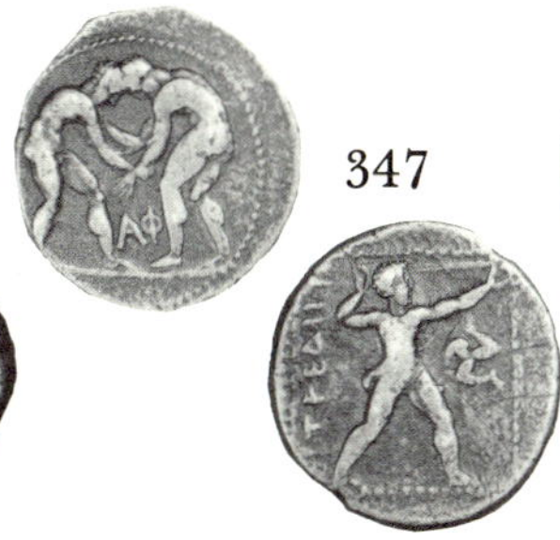
347

348

349

350

351

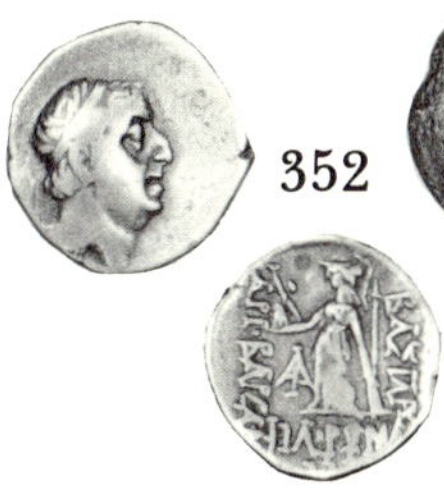
352

353

354

355

356

357

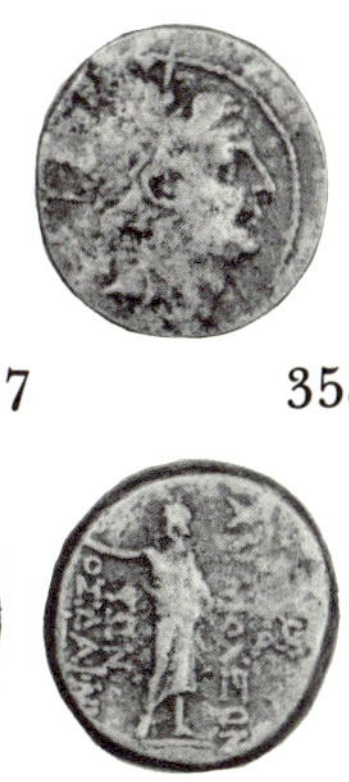
358

359

360

361

362

363

364

Plate 19

365 366 367 368 369

370 371 372 373 374

375 376 377 378 379 380 381

382 383 384 385

THE JOHN MAX WULFING COLLECTION

386 387 388 389 390

391 392 393

394 395

396 397 398 399 400

THE JOHN MAX WULFING COLLECTION

401 402 403 404 405

406 408 410 411 412

407 409

413 414 415 416 417 418

THE JOHN MAX WULFING COLLECTION